Prologue

I am in my little basement wood shop running some boards through my planer to bring them down to seven eighths of an inch thickness. After this, I will run them through the jointer to get one straight and true edge. Later, I"ll rip them to size.

Now, though, I have to first sit down and rest my aching back. As the years go by and my back grows worse, I spend more time in my shop sitting down rather than doing much woodwork.

Sitting down at regular intervals like this gives me time to dwell on memories and musings. Why are things as they are? What were things like years ago? What if someone would change a couple of key things? Could life in our country be better?

I

Dad died suddenly in nineteen fifty two. Now, more than sixty years later, he wouldn't recognize life in our country. Personal computers, cell phones, digital watches, color and 3D television as well as jet passenger air service were unknown back in his day.

I am sure that the election of Barak Obama to the Presidency as well as the numerous and profound social changes that have taken place would simply amaze him. I don't think that he would believe that a woman is secretary of state and that there was an Afro-American serving as chairman of the Joint Chiefs in the pentagon. Yet I don't think that these differences would surprise him as much as the change in the status, power, prestige and living standard of our country today.

I remember walking with him down McClellan street where we lived in the Bronx. He was explaining to me why the new model cars no longer had running boards. Today, I confess, I no longer remember his explanation. I do remember, however, almost every make of car that was being sold then. A customer could buy a Hudson, a Packard, a Studebaker, a Kaiser, Frazer or Henry J, a Nash, a De Soto, a Crosley, a Wiley's, a Pontiac, an Oldsmobile as well as a new Plymouth. Along with all these brands of automobile you could also buy a new Chevy or Buick, a Cadillac or Dodge, Chrysler or Ford, Mercury or Lincoln as you can today.

What you couldn't buy, however, was a Toyota, Nissan, Honda nor any Japanese car; no Hyundai nor any Korean car; no

Mercedes, BMW, Hitler's Volkswagen nor any other German vehicle; no English nor French cars; no Italian cars. Folks, at least some of them, did know that some of these European cars existed, but no one actually saw them. No one in their right mind would ever consider buying one even if they could be found. Only a crazy person would trust his life, or his family to some foreign made thing.

Not only was automobile manufacturing an order of magnitude more expansive and greater than today's shadow of what once was, but there was continual maintenance and modernizing of the roads, bridges and tunnels that they depend on. It is true that we have more of these public facilities today, but we also have nearly double the population along with a vastly higher percentage of the population owning and driving cars. Almost daily the news media reports of bridges being inspected and found unsafe. Roads frequently are almost unusable due to pot holes and crumbling pavement. Modern day motorists are accustomed to driving through disgusting, filthy tunnels.

Back then, as today, vehicles as well as most every other type of merchandise and raw material was sent to and from foreign lands by ship. At that time most trans oceanic transport of vehicles was from the U.S. to other countries, rather than from them to us as it is these days. The difference that I would like to point out however, is the ships themselves. In 1952 almost all commercial ships were produced in American shipyards. Today the American shipbuilding industry is virtually nonexistent.

My father worked in an office in midtown Manhattan. He would sometimes have to put in time on weekends. On occasion he would take the family with him into the downtown area. One of the great attractions for me was the Automat. This was a cafeteria chain that had great food, and for me, a fascinating coin operated food dispensing system. I found, however, the most interesting and exiting part of that jaunt was the ride in the subway. One of the many things about this ride that I remember was the plate riveted to the outside of the motorman's cab that had the name of the subway car manufacturer. Usually it was the St. Louie Car Company or A.M.F., (American Machine and Foundry). Today one can take that same ride, but the plate on the motorman's cab will read, "Bombardier". Bombardier is a Canadian manufacturer of light rail and subway cars. In the U.S. this industry has all but disappeared.

How would a person travel from Los Angeles to San Francisco in nineteen fifty two? Then, as now, the distance could be driven, or one could buy a bus ticket or board an airplane. By far, however, the most pleasant, efficient and practical transportation was provided by railroad. The train would take passengers from city center to city center. Comfortable, pleasant and efficient rail service was used to connect not only the large population centers of major cities, but almost all towns and villages were connected by rail.

The United States became a major economic force in the

world mainly through the construction and development of her extensive passenger and freight rail system. Our freight trains continue to run today, but what has happened to what was the best railroad passenger service in the world? Today travelers who return home from Europe rave about the railroads they experience there. The bullet trains of France and Japan are world famous. Germany is developing advanced mag lev rail systems using magnetic levitation instead of the conventional steel rail and flanged wheel system still used here. High speed rail service connects the cities of Japan and Europe and has been doing so for years. A cooperative effort between France and England has produced the Chunnel; a railroad tunnel under the English channel. This was an enormous project that the people there felt justified the tremendous cost and effort to produce. It appears that they were correct as there is now rail service between London and Paris. This service has proven to be efficient and comfortable and therefore popular and profitable. This and other European, Japanese and now Chinese railroads exist because of the participation of their respective governments.

Light rail and trolley service was used extensively to connect urban downtown areas of major cities to outlying areas as well as connecting smaller population centers to one another. These transportation systems were quiet, clean and efficient. By and large trolley and light rail systems no longer exist in the U.S. Inner city trolley service has been replaced by diesel busses and outlying suburbs are mostly connected by roadways. Those areas that retain rail service have seen their service become obsolete and inadequate. Case in point, the infamous Long Island Railroad. In Europe light rail and trolley service has been well maintained and carefully developed over the years so that their systems are modern and work well.

Today our local transportation situation is abysmal. Many people without cars cannot easily get to work, to stores, to visit family members or for the myriad of reasons people find it necessary to travel about. Those who do own cars run into an ever increasing traffic nightmare caused by the disintegrating roads, bridges, etc. and by the fact that the automobile is often the only transport available. Despite all of the progress made by the EPA, our air quality remains poor because of the fumes spewed out by the unnecessary automobile traffic as well as diesel exhaust produced by all of the busses being used.

This is by far not the only ramification of our backward and neglected transportation and associated manufacturing situation. Our poor passenger transportation systems also affects movement of freight and of raw materials as well as manufacturing supplies. This is due to increasing automobile traffic congestion which increases shipping costs helping to raise the cost of American made goods both domestically and abroad.

One of the once great American industrial enterprises was the steel industry. To be successful any industry depends on its customers. The steel industry relied on sales to shipyards, light rail manufacturers and especially to our huge auto industry. With the great reduction in the customer base for the steel industry the opportunity they provided for employment and the development of careers has dried up.

Let's for a moment think of the manufacture of cars, ships and trains. To produce these things factories need supplies. Therefore, huge amounts of stuff must be shipped to these factories. For these factories to exist, they must send the products they make to their customers, or their dealers or distribution centers. What happens if all this shipping is greatly reduced or eliminated because of reduced manufacturing? What happens to all of the people that had careers with these shipping companies? What happens to the people who had careers with the companies that sold stuff to the shipping and freight companies?

What does a manufacturer need to make a car besides steel? Because cars are still principally made of steel and because they must be made attractive, they must be painted. A huge quantity of paint is used in the manufacturing of automobiles. Needless to say, as American automobile production shrank, so did the production of paint. Along with the cut back in paint manufacture, was a reduction of the ingredients used to produce paint. Chemicals used for pigments, vehicles, binders, drying agents and solvents are less in demand. Less in demand also is the machinery used to blend, store, and package paint, paint ingredients and related products.

Cars, however are not just steel and paint. Each vehicle requires miles of copper wire as well as huge amounts of plastic. Many car parts are made of aluminum. Glass windshields, back lights and side windows must be made. Cushioning, fabric and thread for upholstery is required. This, I am sure, just scratches the surface of what must be shipped to an automobile factory. We have not just lost an enormous part of our auto industry, but also a large part of those businesses that produce and ship all that the auto industry buys in order to produce their products.

In recent times, the sale of imported vehicles have been steadily increasing while the sale of domestically built cars have steadily decreased. Things got so bad for the American automobile industry that Chrysler and General Motors were on the verge of disappearing. While the President of the United States was involved in arranging huge loans to keep those companies alive other political notables were complaining that this bail out would mean that the federal government would be running General Motors and that would amount to socialism. Conservative politicians advocated letting these companies go under in order to preserve our capitalist economic system.

The executive branch prevailed in this dispute and General Motors got public funding in order to remain in business. There were caveats to this federal loan. G.M. could only operate with federal oversight. The government insisted that the company

8

clean house. First by removing the former, incompetent company management and installing a completely new leadership. Also, the government felt the company to be bloated and too large to be profitable. Therefore, poor selling and redundant General Motors brands such as Saturn, Pontiac and Oldsmobile were dropped. Completely redesigned models along with better engineered models from European divisions were put into production here and badged as Buick, Chevrolet and Cadillac. The result of this was unbridled success. G.M. has since repaid their loans with interest, making money for the public coffers and is once again independently run. But, more significantly, all the ancillary industries that supplies General Motors are also up and running.

What could have been the possible result of the failure of the Government to act to resurrect G.M.? The disappearance of General Motors would have resulted in the sudden termination of thousands of jobs. The companies whose business it is to supply the auto manufacturer with everything needed for production could not have remained in business for long with such a loss of demand for their products. This, of course, would have resulted in the loss of many more jobs. Railroads and trucking companies involved in transporting freight to and from those auto plants would have also lost significant amounts of business resulting in further job losses.

The loss of General Motors' suppliers would have made it difficult if not impossible for Ford and Chrysler to obtain the materials they need at reasonable prices and in a timely fashion. It is unlikely that these two manufacturing giants could have remained in business under such impossible conditions. Therefore, it is not just the loss of General Motors that would have occurred, but the loss of the entire industry and most of the supply companies as well. Without an auto industry, how effective would our military be if all of its vehicles had to be imported? Would our steel industry still exist? Consider the ripple effect of all the unemployment that would have resulted from such a catastrophe. Markets for other goods selling in the country would suffer because of the vanished buying power from the thousands thrown out of work. Wouldn't the United States be headed for third world status? Our capitalistic economic system, however, would remain undamaged.

Ship building and light rail manufacturing had similar requirements for steel, glass and all the ancillary industries that had kept the auto companies running. This destruction of American industrial output has lead to what is called today, "The Rust Belt". Really what that means is the near destruction of cities throughout what was once the American industrial heartland. What were at one time thriving residential communities are now either abandoned or run down, crime laden areas of grinding poverty. Busy factory complexes employing thousands of people have turned into empty, deserted buildings with broken windows, rust, decay and peeling paint.

While this industrial atrophy was happening here, things in Japan were quite different. At the end of World War Two Japan was a totally shattered land. Virtually all of her manufacturing and production facilities had been bombed into rubble. Infrastructure was also destroyed. Besides the help they got to reorganize from the U.S., the renewed Japanese government was forced to take charge of rebuilding their nation.

The Japanese government decided what public monies were to be spent, where and for what project, and how much was to be budgeted for it. Their government chose the design and checked on the quality of the work performed. It was the government that decided which industries would receive support.

Entrepreneurs began manufacturing and exporting all sorts of products that they made in what they could salvage from bombed out factories. These were cheap, poorly made articles that began to damage the reputation of Japanese goods. The words, "made in Japan", were synonymous with worthless junk. The situation became so severe that even the Japanese people would try not to buy their own domestically made products. Economic growth couldn't be realized without a strong export market for Japanese goods. Exports couldn't be realized unless the perception of Japanese merchandize overseas changed.

In order to improve the situation their government felt it necessary to intervene. To this end they set up special government agencies. These government agencies examined products made for export and allowed only those that passed their quality control standards to be shipped abroad. Gradually as time passed and brand names such as Nikon, Canon, Honda, Toyota and many,

many more to numerous to name became known worldwide as the finest of their type resulting in the greatest economic growth seen anywhere up to that time.

So far two examples of government action in respect to economic endeavor have been demonstrated. The Japanese government and the action of the federal government here in saving General Motors and at least some of our industrial base. It was previously discussed how our country's industrial power was developed around our railroads. It should be pointed out, however, that our railroads were developed by federal action enacted by the Lincoln administration. That President provided the incentive for the transcontinental railroad to be built and for the purchase of extensive rights of way. President Lincoln was truly far seeing as these actions lead inexorably to industrial expansion.

Our trip into Manhattan with Dad was often to his office. He worked as vice President in charge of sales for Summit Mills Corporation. The company had, of course, its main offices in New York City and the factory in an upstate New York town called Philmont. Summit Mills would design and manufacture men's sport shirts which were sold to retailers nation wide. The factory in Philmont was a fascinating place. There were rows of gigantic knitting machines and enormous tables where skilled workers cut stacks of knitted cloth to shape from patterns as well as row upon row of high speed power sewing machines. I remember on one factory visit the knitting department manager taking us to see the new public school complex that had just been built partly from the taxes paid by Summit Mills.

The school which was getting ready to admit students for the first time left a great impression on us all. It was the first time in my young life that I had seen a modern school building. P. S. 114 where I had been attending in The Bronx was a nice, well equipped institution, but not nearly the equal of the Philmont school complex. They had water coolers in the halls where one could get a drink of ice cold, chilled water. They had desks with Formica tops. They had green black boards which left me puzzled as to what to call them.

The factory town of Philmont was neat, clean and well maintained with attractive homes and a busy downtown shopping district. The surrounding area had busy farms and the whole place appeared like a Currier and Ives painting. Summit Mills was in business for years after my father's passing, but finally succumbed to overseas competition along with other mills located in the town. All either went out of business or moved their plants elsewhere. The result of this was that Philmont went into decline as did communities in the rust belt, Because of the beautiful and scenic setting of Philmont it is now experiencing a renaissance due to tourism and housing for wealthy homeowners. This is not true for most other areas of the country where mills have shut down.

A trip through Walmart, Target, Sears or other large volume retailer's clothing departments can be quite revealing. Looking at the labels on shirts, trousers, jeans or shoes to name just a few, will show that hardly any are made in the USA. The apparel industry has seemed to suffer the same fate as the transportation industries.

While foreign auto makers sell their products here, they at least put their own names on them. The clothing manufacturers, however, put American brand names or American sounding brand names on their products. A pair of Nike sneakers, or New Balance shoes will bear labels indicating foreign manufacture. In the case of the automobile, folks turned to foreign brands because of perceived better quality or superior design. Not so with clothes. This was a change that took place for economic reasons benefiting the manufacturers. These were not changes due to customer selection, but changes made without customer's participation or often without customer's knowledge. A shirt could, and often is, designed here but could be woven in Pakistan and assembled in Mexico. These foreign makers often employ children and run sweat shops that have been illegal here for many years.

Our government has done little to alleviate this situation. Tax and other incentives have been proposed from time to time to Congress but not much has been forthcoming. This situation has preserved our capitalistic system while letting factories close, throwing people out of work nation wide.

Televisions, sound recording devices, telephones, copying machines, computers, high fidelity stereo equipment and other consumer electronics were either invented here or have been mostly developed here. Yet almost none are currently made here. The United States had the largest and best consumer electronics industry in the world. Has anyone recently seen an American made television? Most all consumer electronics are made in South Korea, China or Japan. Panasonic, for example, is actually a product of Matsushita electric of Japan. American brand consumer electronics virtually no longer exist. Philco, Zenith and DuMont have been gone for so long that the public no longer remembers that they were among the best selling brands. Most of the American brands that are still available are actually manufactured overseas. Apple and other computer manufacturers whose designs are American are mostly made in China.

Not that many years ago the telephone company was a monopoly. It was government regulated and sold no telephone hardware. They mostly sold only their service which was at the time the best in the world. The telephones that the public used in their homes and elsewhere were leased from the phone company. The equipment was manufactured here by a phone company subsidiary called Western Electric. Since AT&T or its subsidiaries retained ownership of the equipment, that equipment was bullet proof. The entire, huge operation was American. The service today is American, but the devices rarely so. It is not the break up of AT&T that is being questioned here, but the lack of government action in attempting to keep American companies competitive in the manufacturing of telephone devices and equipment.

At home, we received as a holiday gift, a new Kitchen Aid toaster oven. It is made in China. Looking around in a typical American home, how many small appliances are made here? The average home in the U.S. could be equipped with a toaster, a waffle iron a stand or portable mixer, a food processor, a blender, a hot plate, a slow cooker, a steam iron, a vacuum cleaner an electric broiler and many more small appliances. Most, if not all of these things, are imported, no matter what brand name they bear.

Non electrical apparatus can also be found in the average house. For example an ironing board, a folding cot, a file cabinet, a bassinet, a changing table, a play pen, a drying rack for dishes and almost a countless number of other things some of which are made here. However, every year more and more of these things are coming from other countries. In this case also, brand name makes no difference.

How many kitchen utensils are American made? Of all the spatulas, mixing spoons, pancake turners, strainers, colanders, salad spinners, paper towel dispensers, can openers and church keys hardly any are domestically produced. The same applies to cookware. Most all of the pots, pans, griddles and the like, are imported; again no matter if the brand is American or American sounding.

A trip to a hardware store, home center or the hardware department of a large discount store can be revealing. Looking through the shelves of electrical equipment will show these household items to be overwhelmingly imported. Light bulbs which were invented and manufactured here are now imported. So are lamp parts such as switches, sockets and all other replacement parts for all types of lighting. Lamps of all types that were once made here no longer are. Not just lamps, but all kinds of lighting fixtures are manufactured abroad. Other electrical household items once made here are now almost all imported items. including extension cords, surge suppressors, receptacles and receptacle plates, all types of switches and switch plates, and many, many more too numerous to mention.

Not only are electrical items mostly imported, but recently the tools used to work with and install these things are becoming imported items as well, this would include screwdrivers, pliers and crimping tools used to install various kinds of terminals as well as test instruments.

I encountered an example of this recently. A type of clamping plier developed in the U.S.A. and manufactured here for many years is called the ViseGrip plier. About a year ago I was in a local home center. In the store's bargain bin I found an imported locking plier being sold for just about three dollars. It was a copy of the ViseGrip plier. On impulse, I bought it. A week or two later I had occasion to use it.

It proved to be a real cheaply made and unsatisfactory tool. The jaws did not line up correctly. When clamped, it was almost impossible to unclamp. The adjustment screw would jam and the chrome plating was beginning to peel off.

Last week while in my local hardware store, I saw a ViseGrip display. I bought a new plier for about fifteen dollars. All over the blister package was the ViseGrip logo. There was also the logo for Irwin Tools on the package. Apparently the ViseGrip company had been bought by Irwin Tools. When I got the plier out of the package, I saw that the familiar workmanship was present. Stamped in the handle was the ViseGrip logo as well as the Irwin Tools logo. I also saw the word, "original", stamped in the handle as well. Missing, however, was the stamp, "made in USA". Getting the blister package out of the trash and searching all over it, among the list of patent numbers, in four point type, I found the words, "made in China".

It seems as though some filthy rich person, or group of people, bought the ViseGrip company. Did they close the plant in the U.S.? Did they perhaps throw thousands out of work then contract to have the tool made in China? What's worse is that they try to disguise the item as American, even going so far as to stamp the word, "original", on the tool itself.

A further look at hardware store shelves will reveal that hardware itself is now mostly imported. Wood screws, machine screws, nuts and bolts are generally imported items. Mending plates, angle irons, various types of brackets as well as hinges, all kinds of knobs and handles seem to be mostly made elsewhere.

It is not just simple hand tools that are increasingly

becoming imported items, but major tools as well. Foreign brands of portable power tools are becoming more and more dominant in the market. Brands such as Riobi, Makita, Bosch and others are steadily increasing their market share. More disturbing, however, is the fact that American brands are steadily being made overseas by American companies. A careful look at a Craftsman drill, or Black and Decker power screwdriver often reveals that it is actually foreign made.

Being a woodworker, I am familiar with stationery woodworking shop equipment. Many Delta, Craftsman and Powermatic table saws, band saws, jointers and thickness planers as well as other machinery and other makers of machinery carry American name plates, but are not actually American made. Foreign made machinery of all types have been making great inroads in the domestic market. Lathes, milling machines, automatic screw machines as well as printing presses and related equipment are increasingly being imported. Observation at a road building or major construction sight reveals an ever widening use of imported earth moving equipment. Even in the medical profession there is an increasing use of imported equipment such as x ray machines, ultra sound equipment and such.

Why is our domestic manufacturing being abandoned? Why is American capital being used to invest in the growth of foreign manufacturing?

II

The United States entered World War Two with the Japanese attack on our naval base in Pearl Harbor. Hawaii. The U.S. Navy was almost completely wiped out by this action. Our armed forces were totally unprepared for this the greatest armed conflict in human history. The Army, Navy and Marines were drastically understaffed. Worse, however, was our lack of modern weapons and military supplies. Things were so bad that we had to train our troops with wooden, make believe rifles because we didn't have enough weapons. This state of affairs was not to last.

The world back then, including our enemies, the Axis powers, were fearful of what war with us would mean. Admiral Isoroku Yamamoto who masterminded the Pearl Harbor attack, made these feelings known. Among the many statements attributed to him was his admonitions to the Japanese military not to awaken, *the sleeping giant*.

It wasn't our courageous military personnel, nor our great military strategists that so concerned the Japanese and the Nazis upon our entrance into the war. It was our industrial strength. We were able to make commercial ships to transport military supplies faster that the Germans could sink them. We were able to achieve a ten to one superiority in tanks, rifles, mess kits, winter battle dress, machine guns, artillery and everything else needed to win a war. We entered the war as a great power. When the war was won, we were not just a great power, we were the greatest power the world had ever seen.

The war effort was waged with weapons and materials supplied by great entrepreneurs like Henry Kaiser who developed the concept of the Liberty ship. These were commercial freight vessels that carried war materials and troops to wherever they were needed. He devised construction techniques and procedures that enabled Kaiser Shipyards to make these vessels not only in greater numbers than our enemies could sink, but in such great numbers that we were able to supply ships to our allies as well.

Brilliant as Kaiser was, he didn't build these ships. His welders, his steam fitters, his riveters, his engineers, his draftsmen, his electricians to name a few of the many skilled and dedicated workers at Kaiser shipyards that actually won the war. It was the American labor force along with the citizen soldier that won the war. It was the workers who produced all the weapons and war materials that won the day for democracy and turned our country into such a great power.

It is both undesirable and unrealistic to expect the return of the utter dominance of American manufactured goods that we enjoyed in the late forties and early fifties. At the end of World War Two the industrial world was a complete shambles. Even by nineteen fifty two, countries like Italy, Great Britain, France, Japan and Germany to name just a few were barely able to rebuild enough of their industries and infrastructure to satisfy their respective domestic demands, let alone export to the United States. This, in part, was the reason for the complete dominance of American products in the market place.

Competition from foreign made goods can serve to stimulate innovation while keeping quality high and prices down. Now, after our recent government involvement in the automobile industry has achieved success, we have a market in which American made products are competing successfully with cars made in Japan, Korea, Germany, Britain and Italy with others expected to enter the scene soon.

What is troubling, however, is a market in which the United States was dominate in the fifties and is now totally absent, or rapidly becoming totally or nearly totally absent. Now, instead of competing with foreign makers, we have abandoned the markets for the most common of everyday items. What can government do to bring our industry to the point where we will once again be competitive? Should our government follow its own lead and offer stimulus money to aid other industries and other companies? Can the U.S. offer incentives to keep a company's production facilities within our borders?

Is there any historic precedent to government subsidy to private enterprise? During the Washington administration the function of government was being argued, discussed and in many instances, enacted for the first time. In this initial constitutional government our founding fathers considered government participation in industry to be important to the success and growth of the nation. Alexander Hamilton, our first secretary of the treasury, advocated using revenue generated by tariffs to subsidize manufacturing. Mr. Hamilton felt that such subsidies would encourage innovation and invention in the new nation. He supported using government funds to help build roads and canals to stimulate domestic trade. These actions, our first secretary of the treasury reasoned, would eventually turn the United States into a truly independent manufacturing power. In this he was clearly correct. Government involvement made us the greatest power on the planet.

Let's take a hypothetical action to work on a real situation. There are virtually no television sets made in the U.S. today as previously discussed. We still, however, have electronics firms that make other products domestically. Suppose the government were to offer a large, low interest loan to two or more such companies for the express purpose of developing a new, high tech television receiver to be produced here. It would have to be designed to perform at least as well as others currently on the market. It would have to be designed to sell for at least a competitive price. To create customer interest it should be innovative at least to some degree. A large loan and/or government grant combined with our domestic engineering talent should make this possible.

Along with federal monetary stimulus, there could be tax and other incentives to keep production of these new products within our borders and even to promote their sales overseas. There would most likely be argument against such government action.

The first such argument would be the expenditure of public

monies and the resultant loss of public capital. This argument seems specious as we have granted huge tax breaks to the oil industries and various agricultural endeavors for many years. There are large, powerful corporations that now pay little or no income tax. General Electric has been in the news recently as one such example.

Close examination of this argument can reveal some interesting realities. Looking at the expenditure of public funds would require a close look at how these funds would be spent. Enormous public funds have been and are now being spent to sustain our military. The war in Iraq and the war in Vietnam seems to have served little if any purpose. Yet in strictly economic terms they cost the taxpayers a fortune. Such funds spent for armed conflict have mostly a temporary economic benefit. Although it serves to employ people in weapons and other related war production, the result of all this labor has no lasting benefit to society. Thankfully, wars don't generally last very long. Therefore, the employment that war production generates doesn't last very long either.

Much of what is produced for a war effort is destroyed during the conflict, or rendered obsolete because of rapid technological changes in weapons technology. It has been only a handful of years since the end of the Vietnam war. How much of the weaponry developed for that conflict is useable today? It is doubtful that any of the helicopters or aircraft other than the B-52 are still serviceable. Military electronics have changed drastically since then. Our soldiers and marines don't even wear the same battle dress nor ride the same combat vehicles. Do any Americans experience any benefit from this huge amount of material that lies idle or has since been destroyed?

In contrast consider the Brooklyn bridge. When it opened in eighteen eighty three, it was considered the wonder of the age. It employed many, many skilled workers such as iron workers, masons, laborers for digging, riveters, and others. It started an industry in spinning cables for the manufacture of suspension cables that still exists today. Use of this now very old and to some, obsolete bridge, has not lessoned over the years. Rather it has more traffic today then it did back in the 1800's. Years ago it served as a vital link between Brooklyn and Manhattan. Today it still serves as this vital link only now it is a valued historic landmark as well.

Another argument would be that the government has no business interfering with the private sector. Again this is a specious argument as our government has been involved in the private sector for many years. From the time of the first Roosevelt administration to this day private monopolies have been broken up by the government or regulated by the government. Public utilities, the automobile and related industries, and the airlines are just a few examples of private enterprise working with government regulation and oversight.

Government spending has been looked upon by many as a foolish waste that can, if not greatly curtailed, lead to government and public bankruptcy. Is this really the case? Where does this public expenditure go in a well planned project? An example of an enormous government funded and managed project that could compare to a major military conflict in expenditure could be the Tennessee Valley Authority.

During the nineteen twenties and early thirties the Tennessee valley was one of the poorest areas of the U.S. Land was being farmed using the same agricultural methods that had been in place for centuries. Much of the land had been farmed out to the point that it could no longer support crops. Farm production fell to alarming lows along with the fortunes of the people. In much of this huge area there was no electric service available and no industries to speak of. The average family there was living on not much more than about six hundred and fifty dollars annually. Illnesses were running rampant among the populace, especially malaria.

Congress passed a bill and President Roosevelt signed it into law creating the Tennessee Valley Authority in nineteen thirty three. The TVA began to develop fertilizers and train farmers in modern agricultural practice such as crop rotation and pest control. They started building huge dam projects in order to generate and sell electric power throughout the region. The Tennessee Valley Authority became the largest producer of electric power in the United States and remains so to this day.

Today, the TVA is still active and continues to expand its activities by introducing modern, safe nuclear power to the area. The Tennessee valley area is now a modern, clean, healthy and comfortable place in our country in which to live and work. The huge expenditure of public funds that were spent to create the TVA resulted in the industrialization of the area. Countless jobs were created, many of which were and still are jobs requiring a variety of specialized skills. Jobs and careers that command high salaries and result in a local population contributing substantial taxes materialized. This now well established, prosperous, population creates an increased demand for goods and services that have fomented the appearance of many ancillary businesses and industries that contribute to the overall local success.

Over the years there has been many examples of government participation with private enterprise in creating, maintaining, regulating and running major projects. Not just the federal government, but state and local governments as well. The California Department of Transportation is one such example of State Government involvement. What seems to be the best example of local government participation in major projects is the New York City subway system. Built by both private and public effort and run jointly by the city and private companies via lease and other arrangements, it is now among the most important of city facilities. It transports millions of people daily from the outer boroughs to and from the downtown financial and commercial districts. Such a vast movement of people would not be possible any other way. The city could not really exist without it.

The point of all this is to show that this country has had a long history of government initiation and participation in many private enterprises. Projects have been started by private enterprise and taken over by the public sector. Conversely, many projects have been started by government and handed over to the private sector and many have been joint undertakings from the beginning.

Even before our country came into being, while we were still thirteen Crown colonies, there were examples of cooperative effort between the Crown and private enterprise. Combining his position as royal post master with his enterprise as printer and gatherer of news, Benjamin Franklin began the first large news network to appear anywhere. A newsworthy event that happened in Boston could be read about in Williamsburg, Philadelphia or New York in just two or three days. The vast network of public information that Dr. Franklin created along with the royal post helped foment the revolutionary ideas that eventually lead to the American republic.

Even before the formation of the United States of America as an independent nation, the need for economical transport from the Ohio territory and western New York to the eastern seaboard was recognized. There was no practical means to ship the grain grown in these areas to markets in the east or across the Atlantic to European markets. In eighteen seven a canal was proposed to connect the Hudson river at Albany New York to Lake Erie at Buffalo New York by then governor De Witt Clinton.

Construction started in eighteen seventeen and completed in eighteen twenty five. The Erie canal opened western New York to settlement and made New York City the principal port of the United States.

From the time of the Erie canal to the rescue of General Motors, government has been involved with private enterprise. It has been shown here that this governmental involvement is far from a new or recent phenomenon. Rather it has always been part of our history from the very beginning. It has been part of the history as well as present day policy in the entire industrialized world.

There are those politicians and their followers who contend that such governmental action is unwarranted, unconstitutional and will bankrupt our nation. As far as bankrupting the country, it has been demonstrated here, that in fact, it built our nation; and if continued, will advance our national interest even further.

Both the justification and constitutionality of these actions have indeed been provided for in the preamble of our national document. This preamble states, *"We the people of the United States, in order to form a more perfect Union, establish Justice, insure domestic Tranquility, provide for the common defense, promote the general Welfare, and secure the Blessings of Liberty to ourselves and our Posterity, do ordain and establish this Constitution for the United States of America."*

This preamble as stated by the founding fathers of our

nation is the reason that our constitution was written and ratified. It states, in part, that it is intended to promote the general welfare. Is that not what the government actions discussed here have done? Why is it that large segments of the population are in opposition to joint participation of government with private industry and investment despite the long and successful history of this cooperation?

III

National as well as state laws, policies and practice have
taken other steps to promote the general welfare. Various labor
laws have been in force for years protecting the health and
safety of workers. These laws have been protecting wage earners
from abuse as well. The law guarantees minimum wage, paid
vacations, overtime and more. These laws have been important in
assuring equal opportunity for women, the disabled, minorities
and others. Insurance for the unemployed have protected many
from homelessness and even starvation as well as improving the
success of those who produce the necessities of life.

Back in the end of the nineteenth and dawn of the twentieth
centuries there were great abuses afflicting the general public.
Perpetrated by monopolistic business practices of giant
industrial trusts, people were forced to pay exorbitant prices
for everyday commodities such as coal, petroleum products and
more. When Theodore Roosevelt became President of the United
States he took the constitutional obligation to promote the
general welfare seriously by initiating laws that broke up the
monopolies of the trusts. He was so successful at this, that to
this day he is known as the great trust buster.

Abuses existed affecting the public health as well. Buying
food for the table could be a dangerous undertaking. Food
sanitation was often disregarded in restaurants, groceries as
well as fruit and vegetable stores. Butchers frequently sold
substandard and tainted meats. To make greater profits, dairies

would water down milk and add chalk dust to keep the white color.

Patent medicines that had no physical benefit or were sometimes even harmful were sold to the public by various charlatans often referred to as snake oil salesmen. Machines were marketed as cures for every ailment one could think of. They usually used electric shocks to make folks think that they were effective. They were at best, useless.

President Roosevelt acted here also to improve the public health by enacting the Meat Inspection Act and the Pure Food and Drug act in 1906. As this President said, *"This country belongs to the people. Its resources, its business, its laws, its institutions, should be utilized, maintained, or altered in whatever manner will best promote the general interest."*

Government action at this time lead to the formation of the Food and Drug Administration. This federal agency has been active ever since, protecting the health and welfare of the citizenry. It was not just at the turn of the century that this and other governmental organizations have been correcting abuses.

In the late nineteen forties and early fifties, when parents took their kids to buy shoes, most children's shoe stores had a fluoroscope machine. The child, after trying on a pair of shoes, would place his feet in this machine. The machine bombarded the child's feet with x-rays so that the sales person and the child's parents could check for proper fit. This, it was believed, would assure the proper development of the youngster's feet as he or she grew.

What the machine did, in fact, was blast the child's body with harmful x-rays. Not only was the child being harmed by these uncontrolled x-rays, but so were the sales people, the parents and anyone near the equipment or in the store at the time. This wasn't a case of someone trying to make a profit at the expense of others. It was simple ignorance. Government agencies, however, became concerned and began to test the machines. Horrified by the result, they acted to ban the machines, thus saving millions from cancer, birth defects and other radiation caused diseases.

During the nineteen seventies there were advertisements on radio and television as well as the print media for a product called, "Carter's Little Liver Pills". This product had been on the patent medicine market for many years. Now the government began looking at the product more closely. They ordered the manufacturer to stop advertising it. Government agencies said that there were two things wrong with Carter"s Little Liver Pills. First, they had no measurable affect upon the human liver. Second, there was no liver in it nor any ingredient in it that was derived from liver. Therefore, they could not be advertised nor sold as any type of liver pill. The company began to sell the product as, "Carter's Little Pills". I clearly remember their television ads demonstrating that the pills were so little that they would roll through a common drinking straw.

Our government stepped in again and barred the company from selling or advertising Carter's Little Pills. The government's position was that the pills were not significantly smaller than many other common pills such as saccharine sweetener and others. They began selling them simply as, Carter's Pills. However, since they couldn't even show them rolling through a straw, let alone make any other claim for them, they seem to have vanished from the market.

Recently the government has been active in recalling foods infected with salmonella as well as other forms of various contamination. Forcing bad food and medications from the market as well as investigating the sources of contamination has been significant in reducing illness and even death among consumers. Yet there are those who would reduce the government's authority to act in this way. Considering themselves conservatives and strict interpreters of the Constitution, they simply disregard the preamble of the Constitution itself.

In 1929 brokerage houses would require only a ten percent margin on stock purchases. This meant that one could buy ten thousand dollars worth of stock by putting up only one thousand dollars. When the value of stocks began to fall, the brokerage houses called in their loans. Because the value of the stocks fell far below what people invested, these loans could not be payed back and the market collapsed.

Businesses took huge losses in their investments and went bankrupt in droves. The masses of boarded up, closed companies caused millions to be thrown out of work which led to the great depression and one of the worst times this land has ever seen.

As the economy contracted, the banks that had held much of the nation's worth began to experience massive withdrawals. Banks began to fail in large numbers as they could not stop the money hemorrhaging from their many closing accounts. As banks began failing the public lost more confidence and withdrawals accelerated. This became known as, "runs", on the banks and caused bank failures at an unprecedented rate, which in turn caused further contraction of the economy.

This disaster eventually led to the formation of the federal Securities and Exchange Commission which has been established to protect the public from financial abuses. While in years past the SEC along with other state and federal agencies have done much to protect the general public from predatory financial practices, for reasons to be discussed later, they have recently been much less affective.

New banking laws and regulations were also fomented by the Roosevelt administration. Among them was the creation of the Federal Deposit Insurance Corporation, (FDIC). Now, depositors could be confident that their life savings were secure in a bank because the federal government was backing it.

In the years just prior to the financial collapse of 2008, the major banks were handing out mortgages for huge mounts of money with little regard for the homeowner's ability to pay. They would then sell blocks of mortgages and purchase other blocks of mortgages creating a market similar to the stock or commodities market. They would actually bet on the rising or falling value of their blocks of mortgages.

Financial deregulation of banks and investment companies in the late nineteen nineties allowed many institutions to become over extended and fail. However, it was felt that if the major financial institutions were left to fail the result would be a catastrophic economic disaster worldwide. Therefore, in 2008 huge bailouts were supplied to these companies by the government.

Banks are being so under regulated and under supervised that today foreclosure regulations are frequently ignored causing many to be thrown out of their homes with improper paperwork. Government monetary grants to banks, designed to provide for mortgage negotiation which could keep people in their homes, is ignored.

The result of this is that banks are taking over unsaleable, foreclosed houses which they then leave abandoned. Also, many are simply walking away from their homes that are worth less than their mortgage loans for which the banks refuse to negotiate. Sometimes the banks that refuse negotiation are the same institutions that accepted government money given to them for the express purpose of lowering mortgage rates to prevent this tragedy. These abandoned houses are left to be vandalized. Light fixtures, plumbing, wiring, heating systems and other built in features of theses houses are being ripped out by desperate people trying to get money by selling these things. This results in a further decline in home values in areas where this is occurring. All the protection the population has enjoyed just a few years go by government participation, law and regulation seems to be disappearing.

Funding of higher education has been supplied by both the major banks as well as the federal government. Those student loans provided by the national banks have become a trap for our youth. Many who are attending school to learn a profession, find themselves in debt to the banks for huge amounts that they often have no way to pay off. The conditions set for these loans are frequently onerous. Even bankruptcy cannot provide any financial relief. As bank executives grow wealthier by the day, many college graduates are stuck in menial jobs while trying to pay loans of eighty thousand dollars or frequently much more. So far nothing has been done about this problem presumably because a solution will not contribute to the increasing wealth of the banks.

During the last fifty years credit cards have become an ever increasing way of paying for most everything. The credit card issuers along with their associated banks have used deceptive advertising as well as deceptive promotions to lure unsuspecting segments of the population into serious debt often resulting in bankruptcy. These companies have been repeatedly accused of directing their promotions and advertising to appeal to the young and inexperienced segments of society. Young college students, military personnel and other similar groups have been lured into crushing debt by such practices.

Credit card companies have engineered their credit agreements so that they can extract interest rates that in years past would have been considered usury. They have couched their agreements in such complex legal terms that even lawyers have difficulty understanding them.

People have often asked Congress to enact laws and regulations that would require credit card companies to disclose their credit practices and print their agreement in type large enough to actually be read and to couch these agreements in understandable terms. Since these companies have accumulated enormous wealth, they have been successful in partly defeating such attempts through a careful campaign of selective political contribution.

Those politicians that have been bought by huge corporate contribution have often justified their stance by blaming the victims of credit card and bank abuses, claiming that the public must become more active and knowledgeable about their agreements. They have compared the arguments for regulation as an attempt to turn the country into a socialist state. The position of many of the so called conservative political groups is to reduce, or better, eliminate many of the federal regulations designed to protect the general welfare. Included in their agenda would be to reverse anti-pollution laws including the dissolution of the Environmental Protection Agency in an attempt to aid the profit making ability of energy companies and others.

One of countless examples of the importance of anti-pollution regulation is the case of the Love Canal. The Love Canal was a residential area of Niagara New York, a city near the upstate Niagara River. The Hooker chemical Company had been dumping industrial chemical waste there for years and finally sold the site to the Niagara School board. When residential construction began, the twenty one thousand tons of hazardous chemical waste that had been buried there was released. The result was widespread illness that was traced to the contamination. This lead to the superfund legislation designed to clean up harmful dump sites nationwide.

The Cuyahoga River in northern Ohio is another example of pollution gone wild due to government inaction. This river has been so polluted since Civil War times that various descriptions of it like, *"this river doesn't flow, but rather oozes downstream"*, or, *"a person falling into this river does not drown, but decays"*. This river was so polluted that it has actually caught fire. Not once, but thirteen times this water was burning. The first time it happened was in 1868 and the last time in 1969 when it garnered public attention. Since then, government action has cleaned it up to the point where it can actually support wildlife and recreational activity.

Air pollution in the U.S.A. and the rest of the industrialized world has grown to the point where we are

39

beginning to damage our planet's atmosphere. The increase in atmospheric carbon dioxide is raising global temperatures alarmingly. The evidence of global heating is obvious not only to the scientific community, but to anyone who is aware of current events.

Horrifying storms, floods, and droughts are occurring with greater frequency and severity year by year. Melting glaciers and polar icecaps are steadily increasing phenomena. Experts are universally attributing this to world wide burning of fossil fuels for energy.

Fossil fuels are the remains of ancient plant and animal life that has existed on earth for more than five hundred million years. We have been burning the dead bodies of animals and plants that have been accumulating for this immense period of time. These fuels are basically carbon which combined with atmospheric oxygen when burned, release huge amounts of carbon dioxide into the air. This material reflects the sun's heat that bounces off the ground, back to the earth raising global temperatures dramatically.

Technology is gaining success world wide in reducing smog and other pollutants produced from burning these fuels. Despite the remarkable achievements in pollution reduction, the fact remains that the production of carbon dioxide grows yearly. The burning of coal and petroleum must produce carbon dioxide. Humanity must find alternative energy that produces no green house gasses. This energy resource exists now and can be

40

developed for use today. In fact, it is being used at this moment.

While conservative politicians and pundits are clamoring for drilling new oil wells, exploring new sources of natural gas and laying new oil pipelines, they are scornful of green energy sources and fight against any public support of wind, solar, water or geothermal energy production.

The argument that conservative forces present is that wind, water and solar power is not consistent and therefore unreliable. When the wind doesn't blow and the sun doesn't shine, green energy production falls. However, when the sun and wind are being tapped, they can produce enormous amounts of electrical energy, more than can be readily used. If only we could store that power for use during periods of low production our problem could be solved. It has, in fact, been solved for some time.

It is easy to convert electrical power to hydrogen gas by electrolysis. In short, this is the process of passing an electrical current through water. From this process we can accumulate hydrogen gas. When green energy methods produce excess electrical power, the surplus can be used to produce hydrogen. This can be burned as fuel when needed. When burned, hydrogen produces pure water and nothing else. The hydrogen produced can also be converted back into electrical current by the use of fuel cells. All that's needed is government investment and participation.

The vocal right are correct in asserting that our country should be energy independent. But they insist that it be done with finding new sources of fossil fuel. They rail against government participation in clean energy projects. Such participation they argue would increase the national debt. However with a joint government/private enterprise to develop new energy, new technologies will be developed as well. A new and marketable American technology could be sold world wide and create a new American industry while solving problems with both energy supply and global warming.. Why are we stagnating in this endeavor?

The American petroleum and coal producers have enjoyed special tax and other government perks. They have accumulated such enormous wealth that through their lobbying efforts and especially through their political donations they have bent government policies to their own benefit. The reason that politicians on the right fight attempts to modernize fuel production is because oil and coal companies have influenced them.

The claim that the use of public funds to modernize our country is wrong, harmful and unwise is as fallacious now as it was during the formation of the Tennessee Valley Authority and the construction of the Hoover Dam. It seems that the only way to our country's future is by separating money from government.

It has even been suggested by conservative politicians that child labor laws be eliminated permitting the hiring of children to clean their own schools, including latrines, furnace rooms, etc.

At the turn of the century there appeared various attempts to restrict the hiring of children to do adult labor. Nationally, the Keating-Owen Act was passed by Congress in 1916 but was found to be unconstitutional by the Supreme Court.

Finally by 1938 President Roosevelt helped initiate the Fair Labor Standards Act protecting American children from often dangerous jobs in frequently unhealthy environments and freeing them to attend school. Today, it would seem, some conservative elements would reverse this progress bringing back the sweat shops of years past.

These positions that the conservatives have taken, they claim, is a conservative and strict interpretation of the Constitution. However, a strict interpretation of our Constitution must include the preamble which the framers considered to be the very purpose of the document. This, in part, charges the government with promoting the general welfare. The promotion of the general welfare is the reason for the enactment of anti-pollution and child labor laws as well as regulations restricting financial abuse.

When my father was explaining why cars no longer had running boards, there were many other differences in those automobiles from the cars of today. Many of these differences were due to the natural change of style and technological advance during the ensuing years. Many others, however, were due to government action.

The cars of 1952 had what is called hydraulic brake systems. When the brake pedal is depressed it forces a plunger down a cylinder which in turn forces a liquid through tubes to each wheel where it applies the brakes. But, if a crack, or a hole, or a leak for any reason occurred anywhere in the system, the liquid would be forced out leaving the vehicle with no brakes. The government decided that this was a dangerous state of affairs and mandated that manufacturers provide cars with dual brake systems.

Today, brake pedals push two plungers. One supplies fluid to the front brakes while the other applies the rear. If a leak occurs brakes will still work on two wheels.

There have been many, many changes to automobiles due to government safety regulation. In part they include, soft, padded instrument panels, collapsible steering columns, progressive crush zones in car bodies, brake lights and other lighting standards, seat belts and air bags, windshield washers, infant and child seat requirements, secure door locks and much more including anti pollution standards for engines. All this and more is enforced by the National Highway Traffic Safety Administration, (NHTSA), a part of the United States Department of Transportation.

Isn't it strange that our country has grown to be a global super power during the hundred years or so of growing government regulation of the private sector. Isn't it also strange that during that same period of time and due also to government regulation, public health has taken a great turn for the better. The fact that property loss, injury and death by fire, traffic accident, industrial accident as well as both chemical and biological contamination have seen a dramatic decline; and yet, despite all of this, popular sentiment seems to be turning against the very government action that has improved so many lives so dramatically?

IV

As discussed, the United States Government has been serving to improve the general welfare of the American population by acting to protect people from health hazards, as well as avoidable accidents on the job, at home and while traveling. Government legislation and enforcement has freed the people from fiscal, job related, and legal abuses and has acted to protect our environment as well.

These, however, are not the only actions that our government has taken to improve the general welfare. The private sector has often created magnificence and achieved greatness in many ways. The private sector, however, has never managed to achieve any kind of permanence.

It is only by the restrictions and regulations imposed by government that private sector achievements can be preserved for the general public who have actually funded what has been achieved by private interests. The public funded them through special industrial and corporate tax loopholes and deductions that permitted the funding for them. Public funding was also supplied through the purchase price of the commodities and services that are being sold to the general population. This commerce has created these powerful interests in the first place.

For many years one of the most influential and wealthy commercial enterprises was The Pennsylvania Railroad. It, along with the Grand Central Railroad, dominated passenger service and

46

more importantly commerce in the eastern U.S. These two railroad empires serviced the metropolis of New York City bringing passengers and almost all freight in and out of the city.

In order to display their wealth and power, these railroads built the most spectacular, beautiful, and expensive stations in New York City that they could.

These two railroad stations called, Grand Central Station and Penn Station were recognized as landmark examples of architectural excellence. These two spectacular structures were part of the city's skyline and midtown Manhattan's color and tradition.

After some time the impermanence of private endeavor began to appear. The construction of the interstate road system made truck transport and passenger car travel cheaper and easier. This combined with the increased popularity of faster jet air travel began to eat into railroad business. As the years went by profits began to turn into losses.

In order to recoup some of their losses, The Pennsylvania Railroad sold the air rights over Penn Station. They were sold to interests that had plans to demolish the station and build a large office complex combined with a new iteration of Madison Square Garden. To sweeten the pot, the railroad received a financial interest in the new complex and a small, free underground station that functions without any ornamentation or any architecture creativity of any note.

The loss of such an imposing landmark was decried

47

worldwide. The New York Times called the demolition of Penn Station, *"this monumental act of vandalism"*. Without government interference, the private sector was free to pursue profits at the expense of the city and the public. The outcry around the city, the nation and even around the world at this vandalism pressured the city government to act.

The furor over the Penn Station vandalism gave impetus to Mayor Wagner who in nineteen sixty five organized The New York City Landmarks Preservation Commission. This government commission has been charged with administering New York's Landmark Preservation Law. Since the law was first enacted twenty seven thousand buildings have been given landmark status along with one hundred seven historical districts as well as over a thousand individual sights and scenic areas all of which are located all over the city. Many of these sights have been recognized as national landmarks and others as national registered historical sights. All this came about to prevent the same vandalism to Grand Central Station as was done to Penn Station. All this just in New York City alone.

All over the United States historical and architecturally noteworthy buildings, sights, battle fields, and districts have been preserved by local, state and federal government action. It is overwhelmingly government action that preserves our art and history.

The general public lives under constant social pressure. The pressures of career, child rearing, taxes, commuting, and paying bills begins to crush the human spirit. People need some kind of recreation to to be able to face these daily pressures.

Many plunk themselves down in front of the TV. When the tube becomes tiresome, folks may go out to a movie, or a show, or a sporting event or even out to the mall for diversion.

If only folks could paddle a canoe on a beautiful mountain stream or lake. If only folks could fish for stripped bass on a beautiful unspoiled beach. If only people could take a hike through a magnificent scenic wonderland filled with wildlife as our ancestors could. This for many people could be the cure for the tensions of modern life. Thanks to local, state and federal government, we can.

Many people find recreation at amusement and theme parks built and run by private enterprise. They have been successfully operating across the country for many years making profits for their operators and fun for people from all walks of life. However they do not provide what government run public parks provide.

All levels of American government have created and are operating and maintaining parks. Some of these public parks are showcases known worldwide. New York City's Central park comes to mind as an internationally renown municipal park. Many people don't realize that the center of mid town Manhattan is fileds with ponds, woods, meadows, and winding paths lined with benches. It's success over the years can be seen by the enormous use that New Yorkers have put to it. There are many concerts held in the park. Shakespeare as well as other dramatic works are often performed there. The big, free park is the center of the city's life.

There are great municipal parks all over the country. Many as spectacular as New York's Central Park. In San Diego, as an example, the citizenry packs Mission Bay Park. With miles of beaches for swimming and fishing, sights for camping, and extensive trails for hiking and bicycling as well. It has become San Diego's main center of recreation.

It is not only major cities across the nation that own and operate successful parks. Smaller communities have parks as well. One of the oldest in the country is in Saratoga Springs New York. A small city of under thirty thousand people it has for years operated Congress Park. A beautiful, unique and popular small urban park.

There are six thousand six hundred twenty four state parks across the country. They vary from Edison State Park in New Jersey that has preserved Thomas Edison's laboratory and experimental equipment to Cass Scenic Railroad State Park in West Virginia that provides rides for the public on antique reciprocating steam powered trains up beautiful mountain railways.

There are wilderness experiences in state run parks nation wide. An example of such a state park is located located in Alaska, called Kachemak Bay State Park. It's mostly sixteen hundred square kilometers of unspoiled beaches, rivers lakes and peaks. There are mostly no roads in the park and visitors must fly in and camp at the wilderness sight they chose.

The most widely known of the public parks in the United States are the fifty nine areas designated as National Parks by The United Sates Congress. These parks are managed by The United States National Parks Service in twenty seven states across the Union. Some of these parks have such spectacular attractions or magnificent scenery that they have become known world wide as some of the most glorious and amazing areas of our planet. Areas that have been and are now being preserved and maintained by government.

It is hard to imagine that the government that has been so devoted to the well being of it's citizenry is the same government that so many people have been arming themselves against for so many years. For so many years they have been armed and organized to defend against a government action that has never come.

At the end of World War Two, the United States Military felt that the general population should have the shooting skills that they had during the eighteenth and nineteenth centuries. Therefore they formed the D.C.M., (The Director of Civilian Marksmanship). Working through the D.C.M. The United States Army sold surplus 30-06 Springfield bolt action rifles to gun clubs across the nation for next to nothing. This was followed by a great give away and sale of Garand M1 rifles to civilian recipients. This was the semi automatic rifle that won World War

Two, became the standard military weapon for most of the nations of the free world and was called by General Patton as the "greatest battle implement ever devised". They also practically gave away twenty two caliber target rifles, spotting scopes as well as other shooting accessories. Thousands upon thousands of round of ammunition were simply given to gun clubs and shooting enthusiasts. This is the government that today's shooters fear will take away their guns. Perhaps they believe their government will come to take away the guns they gave them fifty years ago.

V

It would seem to many that the communist, dictatorial government of Cuba would not be greatly concerned about the welfare of its population. After all, civil liberties and personal freedom have never been the hallmark of its policies. Yet, surprisingly, the health care system of this island nation along with many other countries has been providing much better services for its people than did the United States.

Almost everywhere in the world, governments consider it their obligation to provide health care for their populations either completely or in part. Many feel that health care is too important to be left to private entrepreneurs to provide without careful government oversight and participation. After all, the purpose of private enterprise is to make money. It would seem that it is in the interest of private health care providers to deliver the least care possible leaving them with the greatest profits possible. What are the health care arrangements in other countries?

In Cuba the government provides all health care services free of charge to the entire population. Of course Cuba is a communist society and one would expect this to be the case. What about other, capitalist nations?

In France, for example, almost all of the health care costs are born by the French social security system. A patient pays little for hospital stays, doctor's visits' specialist consultations, dental or ophthalmology care. Patients pay almost nothing for pharmaceuticals. The cost is covered by compulsory contributions from employers and employees. France, it is said, has the world's best health care system. France also has the most expensive system in Europe, although it is substantially less expensive than The United States has been.

In England health services are provided by the National Health Service. This service is supported by general tax levy and provides most health and dental services as well as medications free of charge to the public. Private services exist and are generally funded by private insurance companies. Only a small part of the English public uses privately funded health services. There have been some problems associated with the National Health Service; especially with finding highly specialized services which may result in long waiting times for treatment. However it highly unlikely that any of the British public would prefer a system like ours.

The Japanese health care system consists of eight different insurance plans. Citizens are compelled to join one of the eight plans. The chosen plan covers seventy percent of the patient's total bill. The cost of patient care in hospitals and medical offices is strictly government controlled.

Our capitalistic neighbor to the north has a mostly government supported health care system. All necessary health services are universally free or in some cases nearly so. Patients mostly do not have to be in any way involved in billing. Services are paid by the government according to a schedule set by law. As in all medical arrangement there are problems. Yet, nevertheless, Canadians support their system by a majority of more than eighty percent.

Dutch medical care is funded mostly by private, non profit insurance groups. Participation is mandatory. The government regulates both the benefits and the premiums charged. Long term care for the elderly as well as the chronically ill are supplied by the government and funded by tax levy.

The World Health Organization has rated the Italian medical system as the second best in the world behind France. Their system is run mostly by a Government agency called the, Servizio Sanitario Nazionale, (SSN). Most health care costs are provided by the SSN either free of charge or fees are adjusted according to income.

In Sweden the health care system is government run and funded through taxation. Medical and pharmaceutical costs are limited. Generally a fee of approximately twenty one dollars U.S. Covers all the costs of a hospital visit. This fee is charged for every doctor's office or hospital visit until the patient has paid approximately one hundred eleven dollars for the year. After this, all medical costs are free for the rest of the year. Prescription drug costs per year are limited to two hundred forty nine dollars annually. Once this cost has been reached, the government pays for all medication for the rest of the year. All pharmacies in Sweden are linked. Patients are issued health care I.D. cards and with this they can obtain their prescriptions at any pharmacy in the country at any time.

Comparing this sampling of medical systems in other countries to what ours has been can reveal some interesting details. According to the United States Census Bureau, over fifty million residents of our country had no medical insurance in 2009. More money per capita has been spent on health care in the US than in any other country in the world. A five state survey in 2001 concluded that over forty two percent of bankruptcies were attributable to health care costs. In 2007 this figure jumped to over sixty one percent. Life expectancy in the US was ranked fiftieth worldwide by the World Health Organization. We were the only nation in the industrialized world that didn't have some sort of universal health insurance for its citizenry.

We are also the only nation in the industrialized world where health insurance is provided by employers. Only in America did the loss of one's job mean the loss of health coverage. When thought about, it becomes plainly apparent that this system was sheer lunacy.

Employers in the US had to pay much more for health care coverage for their employees than those in other countries. This resulted in higher manufacturing costs. This high cost of medical coverage in our country affected our ability to compete with foreign manufacturers of consumer goods and therefore our national economy suffered. It is one of the reasons for there being such a high percentage of foreign made goods in our markets.

Many here in the U.S. have advocated initiating a single payer system to provide health care for the general public as is done by other countries like Canada and Sweden, for example. Lobbyists in Congress so far have been successful in dissuading politicians from even presenting such a bill from being seriously discussed. The fact that Medicare and Medicaid are basically single payer systems that have been operating successfully for many years and have been viewed most positively by those who have been depending on them, have been disregarded. So also has been the Veteran's Administration which provides health care for retired military personnel under complete government control and funding. There are other government medical plans that have been working as well.

Other plans have been considered that retain private insurance with compulsory coverage of those who have preexisting conditions as well as other corrections of previous health care deficiencies. Under this type of plan which which is in operation in the states of Massachusetts and Hawaii and has been recently enacted into federal law after great Congressional turmoil.

This plan has part of the cost of an improved system being covered by an increase in the number of participants. This increase in participation is realized by mandating coverage for the majority of the population. Many have objected to mandatory insurance claiming that it is unconstitutional. However, courts including The Supreme Court have upheld the provisions of the new plan. Conservative politics has uppermost in its agenda the repeal of health care reform and a regression to the previous disastrous policies.

Conservatives have presented arguments against the single payer system as well as against most any other type of real health system reform. One of these arguments is that the government has no business getting involved in the private affairs of the health or insurance industries. But this argument seems to run aground when one thinks of the Veterans Administration and the other single payer systems that had been in use for years. Also, it seems clear that such government involvement is about promoting the general welfare as written in the Constitution.

Another argument against governmental health care is that it is a socialist system. Now that it is enacted, the argument goes, our country has become more like the socialist countries of Scandinavia, like Sweden, for example. Who wants that to happen?

If an economic system is desirable it seems to depend on how well it works. How well an economy works, seems to depend on how well it provides for its population. It would also be a system in which personal freedoms and liberties can flourish.

Well then, what about Sweden? They seem to have a modern, efficient and high quality health care system. But how do they live under the crippling poverty, the innovation and creativity stifling effects of their socialist system? While in Stockholm, I looked for people to speak to about this in the city's slum areas. I failed because I couldn't find any slums. What I did find, however, was a neat, clean, well dressed and apparently well fed public. Stockholm looked sparkling and filled with restaurants, boutiques, stores and shops stocked with beautifully designed and made merchandise. The people seem to be enjoying personal freedoms comparable to what we enjoy. Most were happy to speak about their country and were cheerfully proud of their national accomplishments. Is this what we are being cautioned against?

What about the suffering masses who live just to the north of us in Canada? How do Canadians cope with their socialist system? Actually, quite well, thank you. Having spent considerable time in Canada and actually having to use their medical facilities on more than one occasion, I found the service better than what's available in the U.S. in almost every way. They seem to live quite well up there. The only thing that they appear to find lacking in their country, that they seem to seek here in the U.S., is warm weather. Many of them, therefore, spend a lot of their considerable vacation time enjoying the Florida warmth.

Why is it that so many people are afraid of a government administered health care system? They seem utterly against it despite the success such programs have had in industrialized places where it has been introduced? They seem utterly against this until they began to be covered under the government's Medicare program. Why are so many dedicated to the scraping of the President's health care plan without any other system to replace it?

VI

As has been discussed before, the warning that is often used in arguments against government participation in and/or regulation of most any sort of undertaking is that it is socialistic. We are often cautioned that any government run facility of almost any type will turn our nation into a socialistic state like those of Scandinavia.

There are many forms of socialism and many different interpretations of what the word means. Under one type of socialism, the state owns and operates all the means of production and no form of private enterprise is permitted. This is generally called communism. There have been many nations that embraced the communistic form of economic and political systems. They mostly failed and have been replaced with systems similar to our own. China views itself as a communist state. Although at one time it was as purely communist as any country ever was, it is no longer so, and hasn't been for some years. There are in the China of today many capitalistic enterprises that have resulted in one of the fastest growing, most successful economies in the world. The socialism of China is no longer communism.

Another form of socialism is generally referred to as, "market socialism". Again this term has been used to describe various forms of economic systems. It is important to decide how it will be used here. Market socialism in this text is meant as a system in which private, capital generating enterprise determines the bulk of economic activity. This sometimes is augmented by government run and funded activity that serves a vital public need, or can function better with some degree of government participation. In this concept, private enterprise must sometimes function within government parameters if found to be vital to the public interest. An example of this can be found in American regulation of private electrical power suppliers, private pharmaceutical manufacturers as well as numerous other regulation of private enterprise that arose from necessity.

Many feel that the United States of America is a capitalistic nation. Is it? Does a capitalist nation really exist anywhere? In the modern, industrialized world, is there any country that has a completely privately run economy? Are there not government operated postal systems, government operated military establishments, publicly operated or regulated water and power systems, and broadcasting systems? Isn't this just scratching the surface of government involvement worldwide? Although there are differences between Sweden and the U.S., don't they both operate in basically the same way?

Privately owned and operated organizations that make sizable profits are and have been doing quite well in Sweden. Here, in the U.S., we are familiar with some of them. Among the many too numerous to mention are Volvo Cars, Ikea Stores and Tempur-Pedic mattresses, recently sold to an American holding company. This very small sampling shows that there are more things in common between the U.S. and Sweden than there are differences. Private enterprise flourishes in Sweden. Socialist operations flourish in the U.S.

There are many socialist enterprises working in America today and have been operating for many years. They have been discussed throughout this text. To reiterate, Our post office actually predates the formation of our country, as does our military. There is the Erie Canal and the TVA. There is the New York City Subway and the Brooklyn Bridge. There is Social Security, Medicare and Medicaid. This is just a very tiny sampling of the enormous amount of government participation in our economy.

The specious argument that a single payer medical plan, or government project, or new regulation will turn the United States into a socialist country like those in Scandinavia is actually humorous. It's funny because we already are such a country and have been for our entire history.

How has the threat of a socialist activity turned into a public curse word? How is it that so many people agree with those politicians that hold up Scandinavian economies as examples of systems to dread even though they seem to work so well?

VII

It is said that nothing in life is sure except death and taxes. If you're dead, you have nothing to worry about. If you're alive, however, you have taxes to worry about.

Taxes are collected by governments to fund their activities. There are too many different kinds of taxes to permit discussing all of them here. Generally though, taxes are extracted from Americans by all levels of government. There are municipal taxes imposed by the community, village, town or city in which one lives or conducts business. There are taxes imposed by one's county and one's state. Finally, there are taxes imposed by the federal government.

Most taxes are considered to be either regressive or progressive tax systems. Usually all levels of government use both types of tax systems. Generally a progressive tax system is one in which the tax collected is graduated in accordance to the ability of the taxed person or entity to pay. Conversely, a regressive tax is the same for all income levels. Sometimes a generally regressive tax can have provisions to help make it somewhat more progressive.

An example of this can be sales tax. This is a tax imposed on the cost of merchandise at the point of sale. It is calculated as a percentage of the purchase price. The percentage or sales tax rate remains the same, say five percent for example, for all purchases in the jurisdiction. This same tax rate for all makes it a regressive tax. But to ease the burden for those less able to pay, there are often exemptions for those items considered life's necessities, like food or prescription drugs. This, it is hoped, eases the burden on the less well off. With these types of exemptions it is hoped that most of the revenue will come from the purchase of luxury goods by those who can afford them.

First initiated by the Lincoln administration to pay for the Civil War, income tax is the classic example of a progressive tax. It is, ostensively, a progressive tax because it is based on income. The higher the income, the more tax is due. It is also considered progressive because the tax rate itself varies being a higher percentage of tax due for those who's income is higher.

Income tax is collected by both the federal government as well as several of the states and some municipalities. The tax is collected from individuals based on their personal yearly incomes. It is also collected from businesses based on their yearly profits.

Although income tax originated as an attempt to create a progressive tax system, many have argued that income tax as it is applied today, is not actually progressive. This argument maintains that although the obscenely wealthy as well as large corporations are taxed at a higher rate than the average wage earner, the actual tax that they pay is far lower and as previously pointed out, it has been in some cases zero. This is due for many reasons, among them are; rich individuals as well as prosperous corporations have the means to keep the best tax experts in their employ; many deductions designed expressly for them reduce their taxable incomes significantly; they are in the position to take advantage of many tax loopholes and deductible donations not available to the average citizen, reducing their taxable incomes further.

Today, the highest tax rate is thirty five percent. This means that someone or some corporation that has earned millions, or even billions, is required to pay no more than this percentage of their yearly taxable income after deductions. With all the special deductions and exclusions this leaves their tax obligation actually far lower than this.

There has been several recent efforts to both close many of these loopholes as well as efforts to raise the tax rate for the extremely wealthy. These efforts have been stopped in Congress by conservative politicians. The conservative defense of this Congressional paralysis is their often vocalized opinion that this will limit the funds available to the, "job creators", thus limiting national economic growth. Known as trickle down economics by liberals, its validity is in question.

In nineteen fifty two the highest tax rate was ninety one percent of taxable income. This is much more than double the present day rate. This high maximum tax rate was in place in nineteen fifty five when the Interstate Highway System construction was authorized. During the Eisenhower administration this system was conceived and promoted by the

President as an aid to the national defense. It was built to promote greater efficiency in transporting military supplies around the country. Its secondary purpose was to stimulate transportation and economic growth. It was one of the largest construction projects ever undertaken by the human race.

Unemployment in the period between 1952 and 1955 was far lower than it is today. The conservative position that high maximum tax rates will stifle the economy and inhibit job creation does not seem to hold water. During this post war time people were beginning to actually live better. Roads like the New Jersey Turnpike and the newer extensions of the Pennsylvania Turnpike were constructed. This was also when home construction began to boom and people began buying houses and moving to the suburbs in large numbers.

Those conservatives that are supporters of low maximum tax rates sometimes illustrate their ideas by referring to the Laffer curve. This is basically a line graph which plots tax rates to theoretical government revenue. It starts at a zero percent tax rate, which, of course, generates no revenue. However, it generates hard work and great productivity because all the fruits of labor, risk and investment can be retained.

At the other end of this graph is a maximum tax rate of one hundred percent. This is shown to also realize no government revenue because if all of the reward for labor, risk and investment is turned over to the government there would be no incentive to produce anything by the entrepreneur. The graph is used to show that there is an ideal intermediate rate that will yield the most revenue. Conservatives have often satisfied themselves that the ideal rate is about fifteen percent. However evidence of this seems difficult to find. As shown, there was substantial economic activity during the nineteen fifties when maximum tax rates were in the eighty to ninety percent rates.

In the nineteen twenties Secretary of the Treasury Andrew Mellon influenced decisions to begin lowering the maximum tax rate from the World War One high of seventy seven percent. The rate was gradually lowered through the decade until a low rate of twenty four percent was reached in nineteen twenty nine, which was the year of the great stock market crash and the beginning of the Great Depression. Proof that the lower tax rate caused the Great Depression is not evident. However, neither is there any proof that a high rate would lead to a contraction of the economy.

Among the conservative economic geniuses there are some who strongly advocate a return to the gold standard that was in place just before the Great Depression. These brilliant minds fail to remember that the abandonment of the gold standard was one of the leading factors that was responsible for the recovery. Evidence for that is the fact that nations began to recover in the order that they left the gold standard. For example, Great Briton and Scandinavia left the gold standard earlier than France and therefore began recovering much earlier.

Income tax is not levied only on wages and salary. It is

also levied on investment income. If a person or entity invests money on some sort of venture, then makes a profit from the venture or the sale of the investment in the venture, this is taxed as income. Currently, investment income is taxed at fifteen percent flat rate. The fifteen percent rate applies if the income is twenty dollars or twenty million dollars. This does not seem to be a progressive aspect of the income tax law. Tax on investment income was much higher in years past when economic growth was quite high. Many of the obscenely rich manage their affairs so that the bulk of their incomes are generated from investment and taxed at the lower fifteen percent rate.

Now these same great conservative minds who advocate a return to the gold standard are advising us to allow extremely rich individuals to have a lower tax rate than their secretaries. Some may actually believe their own nonsense

The current tax rate was initiated during the Bush administration. Those who advocated cutting the maximum tax rate said that it would increase government revenue. They cited the Laffer curve as one of their arguments to support this tax cut. As previously pointed out, there is no evidence to support this contention. In fact, since this lowering of tax on the wealthy and corporations, revenue has not been increased. Rather, the same conservative, wealthy elements are now decrying the huge public debt. The solution that they advocate is to cut government services to the lower and middle income populations while they push for lower taxes for themselves.

Revenues for the extremely wealthy minority has increased astronomically in recent years. Jobs, however, continue to become scarce. More and more manufacturing is being done overseas in order to maximize profits for investors while more and more American workers are loosing their jobs. What has happened to the American job creators? The wealthy exporters of American job opportunity and manufacturing careers pay a smaller percent of their incomes for tax than do the people that sweep out their offices.

Why have the job creators failed to create jobs? The answer is that they are not job creators. They are profit creators. Their purpose is to create profits for stock holders. If jobs must be created in order for them to make profits, they will. Most often, however, profits are maximized when jobs are eliminated. If a product can be more cheaply produced overseas then that will realize a greater profit and no jobs will be created here. Who then are the job creators?

There is an economic natural law that is far older than the Laffer curve or most any study in economics. It is the law of supply and demand. The demand is the desire of a significant number of people to posses an item and have the means to buy it. The greater the demand, the more that the item will cost. If there is a great supply of these items, then these products will cost less. The demand for products like shirts, telephones, tuna fish, televisions and so forth is created when there is a large population that wants these items and can pay for them. This is, of course, the working public with disposable income.

Imagine a CEO of a large manufacturing concern. Imagine this person hearing the news that the maximum tax rate has been increased from thirty five percent to thirty nine percent. His company is running at capacity with just the right equipment and the right labor force to just fill all of the orders for his products. But, because his tax rate has gone up four percent, he decides to lay off five percent of his labor force. The fact that he can no longer fill the orders he has for his product and is seeing a loss in business revenue will not matter to him. Really!

On the other hand imagine this CEO hearing that his tax rate has been cut by four percent. His well managed factory is running at capacity with his labor force at the right size to fill all the incoming orders for his products. But, because his taxes have just been lowered four percent he decides to hire five percent more workers, even though some will have to be paid for standing idle. Really!

What would persuade a manufacturer to hire more workers and purchase more equipment for his production facility? Less taxes would have, perhaps, some affect, but would more people be hired because of it? Would reduced taxation persuade a company to hire more workers to produce goods for which there is no market? If the company's taxes were somewhat higher but there was an increased demand for the company's goods; if there are more orders for their products than their current labor force can produce; wouldn't the company be forced to hire more workers to fill their new orders? The new orders, of course, would come from the increased buying power of the general public.

Let's take a brief look at unemployment insurance. Decried by the wealthy and many conservatives as a government handout to the lazy and indigent, it is actually an insurance plan paid for by employers. This type of insurance plan is paid for by taxes levied on employers by both the states and the federal government jointly. It is usually administered by the states. The lazy and indigent are not covered by this plan because it only insures those who have worked for a sufficient period of time to qualify.

What happens to the funds that are distributed to recipients of unemployment benefits? Unlike the unwarranted tax benefits to the wealthy which are often invested in foreign banks, property or other enterprises outside of our borders, unemployment benefit funds are spent within our borders by our own citizens for basic necessities. The bulk of this money goes for food, rent, clothing, transportation, fuel and other items putting money directly and immediately into our economy. Unemployment insurance recipients do more to create jobs in the United States than do the wealthy!

It does not appear to be in the interest of that very wealthy, tiny minority of influential people to create jobs or support a large, prosperous and growing middle income population. This can be illustrated by resistance to a raise in the maximum tax rate of just three percent by the agents of the wealthy in Congress who protested this loudly and often, call it, "class warfare".

The accusation of class warfare inherently recognizes the existence of class in American society. Conservatives seem to prefer a stratified society in which their benefactors are at the top, an aristocracy as it were. They seem to desire that the United States became a caste society that they rule with serfs at their beck and call.

While it may be a wonderful dream to become an American Rajah, it is short sighted and unwise. In order for the new American aristocracy to retain and even increase their wealth and power they must sell goods or services to make profits. One can only sell to one's customers. By actively attacking and reducing the middle income sector they reduce their customer base which in time will actually reduce their profits, wealth and influence.

Having goods manufactured by cheap labor in sweat shops overseas seems to create immediate profits for the wealthy. However, as this process continues and middle income America sinks lower and lower into poverty and the customer base is continuously reduced, the wealthy will most likely move to someplace with a growing middle income. Perhaps to China or to India where their perceived upper caste self image will be more acceptable. Where will this uncontrolled, unregulated rampage of

73

greed leave our nation?

A good example of the attacks on the general public by the obscenely rich is the recent assault on unionized labor, especially against public employees. In order to reduce taxes, particularly the pressure to raise taxes on the wealthy, they have pushed through cuts in state and local government budgets. Arguing that public employees are bilking the public coffers through oppressive union rules, salaries, pensions and health insurance, they have persecuted the public sector making cuts that have created hardship. Hardship not only directly for the affected employees, but for the public as a whole by reduction of services. Ultra conservative governors have been elected to do this through massive political donations from individuals of enormous wealth as well as powerful corporations.

For strictly economic reasons, it is clearly necessary to raise the taxes for the filthy rich. There are, however, other reasons. It is a constitutional obligation of the federal government to strive for perceived fairness in law.

The British colonists in North America picked up arms against England primarily because of unrest over perceived inequality and injustice due to tax inequities. When forming a new, constitutional government, the framers of the Constitution felt a need to write down what is called the, "Preamble". This states the purpose of the American Constitution. The Preamble is the part of our national document that has never, nor ever should be changed. One of the responsibilities of government as laid out by this document is to, "insure domestic tranquility". After a war caused by a lack of domestic tranquility due to public outrage over taxation, the inclusion of this part of the preamble is hardly a surprise. Government is charged with the responsibility of funding public activity, but has the constitutional responsibility to make taxation equitable in order to ensure domestic tranquility. The public perception of unfairness in the current tax laws are beginning to create unrest nationwide. Having a national tax code that has fomented demonstrations sometimes degenerating into violence does in no way insure domestic tranquility.

The filthy rich, it would seem, are clever, deep thinkers, who can justify their insistence for the perpetuation of the tax inequities that they enjoy. However, it is apparent that they really are not so wise. Otherwise they wouldn't defend their privileged tax status with the argument that liberal politicians as well as the liberal media are inciting class warfare by calling for them to pay a more realistic share of the tax burden.

When the privileged cry class warfare, they are acknowledging the existence of a class society in America. In this class society, they seem to say that they are the upper class and the rest of us are the lower class. Perhaps they view our country as a caste society similar to that which is disappearing in India. Are they the maharajas and the rest of us the untouchables? Do their stomachs churn at the thought they

might have to interact with what they consider the great
unwashed?

It is puzzling that large segments of society think that
giving grossly unfair tax advantages to billionaires will help
the general welfare and the finances of the middle income.

VIII

Is there a common thread that runs through all the topics so far discussed here? It seems as though there is not just a spreading resistance to government action, but an effort to repeal laws and undo decisions that have permitted past government participation and effectiveness.

There is pressure from the right to repeal health reform using the arguments that it is unconstitutional, un-American, un-Godly, too expensive, too cumbersome to work and most ludicrous of all has government bureaucrats interfering with the doctor/patient relationship.

Federal courts have upheld the constitutionality of health care reform many times over; most recently by the Supreme court.

If it is legal, done in America by Americans, then it is American. If it is un-Godly, then the Almighty will correct it in His time and in His own way. For whom is the reform too expensive? Is it too expensive for the college student or the student's parents who are to get medical coverage for the first time? Perhaps it is too costly for those patients who have pre-existing conditions and were in the past denied medical insurance. Is it too costly for the almost fifty million Americans who have been unable to afford coverage in the past? For a system that is too cumbersome to work, it seems to work quite well in Massachusetts; and quite well in one form or another across the entire industrialized world. Who in their right mind would prefer dealing with an insurance company bureaucrat with a vested interest in saving his company money over a government bureaucrat who has no such interest?

Why are so many people content to pay a higher percentage of their incomes to the tax collector than does the wealthiest minority? What makes these people think that the filthy rich create jobs when in reality it is the purchasing power of the general public that creates jobs? Why are so many people voting and speaking against their own personal economic interest?

In the past few years the maximum tax rate for the obscenely wealthy has been drastically lowered because, some say, it will enable them as job creators to create job opportunity. Where are the jobs?

There are so many manufacturing facilities closing and jobs disappearing, yet politicians rail against any sort of government action to save them. It has recently been announced that General Motors is once again the worlds largest manufacturer of motor vehicles. Yet, unbelievably, there are some who have sought the presidency that are critical of the successful moves that have saved G.M. and the entire industry from oblivion.

Why are supposedly intelligent politicians denying global warming despite overwhelming scientific evidence of its existence? How on earth can they and their followers think that they know better than the entire scientific community?

In nineteen twenty nine the stock market crashed throwing the country into the great depression of the dirty thirties.

Therefore, strong and effective government regulations were enacted to prevent such a disaster from reoccurring. Yet now, beyond belief, there are pressures to limit government financial regulation and safeguards.

In not many years past, the millions of vehicles on our roads were spewing forth tons of pollutants into the air including poisonous lead oxides from the leaded fuels they were using. Particulate contamination from millions of diesel powered trucks and busses choked the air with foul smelling smoke because, in part, there was very little light rail service. While enormous profits were being made by filthy rich industrialists, asthmatic children were struggling to breathe. Coal fired power generation as well as unregulated chemical plants were helping to turn the air in much of our country almost opaque. The pollution of our lakes, streams, rivers, and shorelines was a national disgrace, as previously discussed.

It was previously written here that Republican President Theodore Roosevelt successfully broke up the monopolies that had been formed by the wealthiest one percent of the population of that time.

The power of these monopolies or trusts were incredible. They would fix the price nationwide of those commodities that they produced. This meant that the consumer had to pay the price asked for the commodity. It was not possible to buy from another source at a lower price because there were no other sources. There were no competitors. Smaller companies were given offers to sell out that they couldn't refuse. When the competition was all gobbled up, then the price would rise to what ever the producer desired in order to maximize profits. The obscenely rich owners of theses trusts began to be called, "robber barons". The name is still used to describe those people today.

In eighteen ninety Congress overwhelmingly passed The Sherman Antitrust Act. This was the first time that the federal government acted to limit private enterprise from killing competition. Without any competitors, the trusts were easily increasing profits at the expense of the general population. Because of the enormous power of the monopolies, nothing was done to enforce this act until the presidency of Theodore Roosevelt.

When President Roosevelt was inaugurated, most of American industry was owned and operated by enormous trusts. These included, the petroleum and petrochemical industries. Standard Oil Company of New Jersey controlled every facet of the industry from drilling oil wells and laying pipelines to ship their products nation wide to retail sales. Control by various other trusts included the railroads and the steel industry from the iron mines to the retailer or builder. They controlled communications, and recently, computer software.

With the breakup of the onerous trusts, control of the country was starting to return to the electorate. However, the robber barons did not disappear. One of the many examples of their presence and influence was Andrew Mellon. Being the third wealthiest man in the U.S. industrialist/banker Andrew Mellon was able to get himself appointed secretary of the treasury in nineteen twenty one. He then successfully promoted the gradual lowering of the maximum tax rate which some maintain contributed to the cause of the great depression.

Despite no longer actually running the country, the influence of the wealthy one percent in government and daily life in is not gone. Actually, our country is now falling back under the control of the robber barons once again. The influence they generate now is much less vulnerable to government control and threatens to become more universal and harmful to our democracy than ever before.

In the past, they began to control the government through their dominance of vital segments of the economy. That was largely coal and oil, steel manufacturing, aluminum production and the railroads to name a few. In recent years the Sherman Anti Trust Act has prevented a return of that type of market domination. An example of this would be the recent government action against Microsoft.

Instead of exercising influence on the U.S. Government through control of vital markets in the economy, the one percent are now exercising direct control of the government.

This is being accomplished in various ways. One means to achieve their ends is by pouring huge amounts of money into lobbyist's efforts to buy the influence of senators and house members in the halls of Congress. The rights of lobbyists is guaranteed by the constitutional right of petition. When, however, does lobbying cross the line into bribery? It is considered bribery when a lobbyist gives money or any sort of gift to an elected official in order to advance his interest. However, is it a bribe to offer funding the election campaign of an official who's political position advances the interest of those represented by the lobbyist?

There have been many examples of legislation that has been passed by Congress to the detriment of the nation as a result of lobbyist's efforts. For years we have had a health system that operated for the benefit of health insurers rather than patients. For years while the general public has been burdened by heavy taxes, the petroleum companies have enjoyed huge tax breaks that enabled them to reap record profits.

To help farmers during the great depression, the federal government instituted farm subsidies. These subsidies once started seem to be never ending. There are situations where farm subsidies are still useful for the small family run farm. But why are the huge agribusiness farming corporations getting more government subsidies now than ever before? Why do their subsidies grow larger year by year while subsidies for the small farm that needs help remains static?

The maximum tax rate for wages and salaries is thirty five percent of taxable income. Someone who is paid two million dollars a year for his or her's uncommon and valuable talent, skill or effort would pay income tax at this rate. Yet one whose income is derived from capital gains or investment income is asked to pay only fifteen percent of taxable income. How many really believe that this actually encourages investment in job creating endeavors? This current investment tax rate is lower now than at any time in recent memory. Now with this low rate the wealthiest among us are becoming rapidly wealthier. Only the wealthiest of us have the means to gain such a huge income from investment because it is they that have the money to invest for income generation.

Most of this onerous legislation as well as onerous inaction has been generated, passed and continued through the efforts of lobbyists. The information and efforts of lobbyists have enabled successful insider stock trading by senators and representatives to rise to unacceptable levels. Those who have been elected to serve the interests of the nation are being forced to resist enormous temptation to serve themselves and in many cases their benefactors rather than the national interest. This is a temptation that is difficult to resist. Many have been unable to do so. Elected officials should be compelled to reveal who the lobbyists that they talk to are, and where their funding comes from. Insider stock trading can be stopped by new congressional rules.

There is, however, a more serious and frightening phenomenon growing in the election process at all levels of government in America. The recent Supreme Court decision that struck down many election laws, some having been in force for nearly one hundred years, have opened a floodgate of special interest funding. By this funding large corporate entities as well as extremely rich individuals have stolen elections and changed government policies to further their own ends. For some reason, large segments of the electorate seems content with this!

IX

Recently, our Supreme Court has decided in the case of Citizens United vs The Federal Election Commission. They decided that,

1. corporations are essentially people and should have basically all the rights of individual citizens.

2. donations to support political candidates and political issues are a form of opinion and therefore equal speech. As speech, they cannot be limited because of the constitutional guarantee of free speech.

This and other recent decisions have fomented the rise of the super pac. This is a political action committee. Its purpose is to receive donations to support a political agenda. This agenda can be to elect an official or to promote or defeat a law or policy.

In the case of an election, under new rules, there can be no collaboration between the pac and the candidate. There are no restrictions on the donor. The donor can be a group, union, corporation, individual or any combination. The identity of the donor and the amount donated does not have to be immediately revealed. Usually not until the election has been decided. Although cooperation between candidate and pac is prohibited, they can communicate through the public media.

The results of this decision have been dramatic.

Politicians with unpopular agendas have received huge donations to support their platforms resulting in many cases to their getting elected. Using nearly unlimited funds they have flooded all forms of public media with frequently distorted and often untrue political advertisement. This has been very notable in state gubernatorial elections of ultra conservative governors and state assembly representatives. These state leaders have been using their offices, as their benefactors urge, to attack labor unions, reduce the public labor force, and cut back on services to the public.

More insidious, however, is the growing conservative political practice of placing obstacles to obstruct the voting of targeted groups of citizens so that the results will be more in their favor. They use a limited strategy of requiring unnecessary, expensive to acquire, approved picture I.D., of changing their state's early voting procedures to create hardship for voters as well as misleading signs posted at polling places. They have in some states created such an elaborate identity check procedure, that the lines at the polls force voters to spend hours trying to cast their votes. All this they say to combat voter fraud. However, voter fraud is not now, nor likely to be in the future, nor ever was a problem in the past.

Under the guise of reducing deficits, and saving state budgets. Their flood of campaign rhetoric, funded by special interests, stressed how they would reduce taxes and by magical means, increase job opportunity in their states.

These states, of course, saw a further shrinking of their economies, a precipitous decline in the quality of public education and a dramatic rise in public unrest and dissatisfaction. With thousands of state and municipal workers now jobless, the considerable purchase power they had is gone. With such a loss of customer base, the markets in these states shrank from reduced sales. This, in turn, caused a dramatic loss of jobs in the private sector.

The public seems to be realizing that they were duped. The outraged electorate is resisting much of the deleterious changes fomented by their new conservative governors and state legislators. There have even been campaigns to recall several of the governors that have been selected by the special interests.

Why has the right wing been attacking organized labor? This conservative program against unions has a dual purpose. The first is the battle between conservative and liberal political forces in the country. The left wing is generally supported and funded by organized labor and middle income organizations as well as lower and middle income individuals. If the power of the unions can be reduced, support and funding for the liberals will dry up.

Secondly, the supporters of the right wing view any union gains as an avoidable and unnecessary expense. This seems to be especially the case with public service unions. Union gains in the public sector, conservatives argue, will cause an increase in some sort of tax. Even the remotest possibility that the filthy rich may have a somewhat larger tax bill is infuriating to them. It is most probably irksome because they mostly don't use public services. Their children attend private schools, they have their own private libraries, beaches, forests, lakes and any thing else one could want.

X

Unions alone have been responsible for the increase in the standard of living from the time of Charles Dickens to the turn of the twenty first century. Much of our modern labor laws emerged out of union pressure and activity.

Today, most of worker's rights are guaranteed by law. This was not always the case. In the late nineteenth and at the beginning of the twentieth centuries, almost no worker's rights existed. Employees worked for twelve, oft times fourteen or more hours daily. They were forced to work in frequently unhealthy conditions. An example of this is the black lung disease suffered by multitudes of coal miners.

Employees were also forced to work in unsafe conditions. Just a few examples of this include the Triangle Shirtwaist Fire of March twenty fifth nineteen eleven. In that fire one hundred forty six young women, most between sixteen and twenty four years of age died. Partly responsible was the company practice of keeping the doors locked so that the women's purses could be searched to prevent pilfering.

One of the most dangerous of occupations is that of coal mining. In nineteen hundred seven there were three thousand two hundred deaths from coal mining accidents alone in that year. Now all mining in the United States is carefully regulated causing the accident rate to drop to about thirty deaths per year. While mining is still a very dangerous job, it is no longer the slaughter that it was before union inspired regulation.

Today there are many government labor laws and regulations that protects the public. Besides health and safety regulations, the public works a five day week and an eight hour day. We are guaranteed by law that working more than that will earn overtime pay. We are guaranteed paid vacations. These and many other worker's rights came from union activity. In reality it was the unions that have created our middle income which has been the backbone of the American economy and American power and influence world wide.

Big business and wealthy industrialists have always been hostile to labor. In the past, the one percent have hired gangs of thugs to break up union meetings, hired private armies to forcefully disrupt picket lines, and have arranged to have union activists assaulted and beaten.

The nonsensical assaults on labor unions have not gone out of style in our time. Rich bankers, industrialists, investors and others have backed candidates for elected positions who rail against unions. They have been blaming unions for every disaster, economic downturn and problem that has ever plagued our nation. Some governors and state legislators have recently been attacking public service unions who represent firemen, police officers, public school teachers and others.

Rights of collective bargaining as well as dues collecting procedures are being rolled back to the labor policies of a hundred years ago. The filthy rich claim that unionized public workers are draining public coffers and throwing states, municipalities and the federal government into irreparable debt. This debt, it is claimed, will cause great damage to our economic future. They say that public service unions have won working conditions, pay scales and benefits greater than comparable workers in the private sector. This, they say, is grossly unfair. They appeal to the public claiming that this inequity is a reason that union gains should be reversed and union activities be curtailed.

With conservative government policy in action, our debt will indeed be reduced. Because of a lack of qualified teachers and closed schools, there will be, along with a reduction in public debt, a reduction in public skill and knowledge and therefore a reduction in available skilled labor. With public employees seeking jobs elsewhere there will also be a reduction in fire and police protection as well as a lack of health inspectors, a lack of consumer protection as well as curtailment of all forms of public service.

The conservative claim that the benefits gained by collective bargaining in the public sector has in some cases created better working conditions, higher pay and more benefits for public workers than private sector workers is correct. This is true because of the weakening of private sector union strength.

Rather than lowering all employee renumeration for their labors to the lowest common denominator, it seems better to raise all to the highest common denominator.

Instead of maintaining that the hard won public sector union gains are an unfair advantage to be envied and challenged by the general public, it would be far better for all if these gains were held up as a goal for everyone.

Why is it that our once powerful and effective unions that have contributed so much to the general welfare are loosing so much popular support?

XI

With the unlimited funds available to conservative causes
and candidates from their wealthy benefactors, they have almost
limitless opportunity for propaganda. The print and broadcast
media are saturated with ads supporting union busting, taxation
inequities and infrastructure neglect.

Because the desires of the obscenely wealthy have such a
tremendous effect on election outcomes, their interests have
governed the actions and inactions of many in Congress. For a
house member or senator to vote against the wishes of their
principal political donors can be professional suicide. This has
resulted in a Congress that has accomplished nearly nothing.
Mostly, legislation has been passed to rename national
monuments, reaffirm the motto, In God We Trust, or some other
generally useless proceedings. Real legislation designed to
address national problems has and is being stonewalled. Why is
this?

Experience has shown that the upper one percent seem to
desire two things, acquiring more money and acquiring power.
These they accomplish in part by reducing their tax obligations
through their influence on election results. Since money equals
power, this is their primary agenda. Through their influence
they have reduced the maximum tax rate on earned income to only
thirty five percent. This seems, at first, to be a reasonable
tax rate, until examined more closely. The obscenely wealthy as
well as corporations actually pay far less than this.

The wealthy one percent actually pay a real tax of about fourteen percent because of the many deductions and loopholes they managed to have written into the tax code. More significantly, they have managed to reduce the tax rate on investment income and capital gains to only fifteen percent. Their political wards justify this by explaining that with more money they will create jobs. This, of course, is a cruel fiction as jobs are really created by the purchase power of the public.

The preamble to our Constitution in part calls for insuring public tranquility. This glaring inequality of taxation is causing great public strife. There are huge public demonstrations for fairness nationwide. A vast movement called the Occupy Wall Street movement has been formed to attempt to bring some fairness back to our national economy. However, due to recently acquired political power, the wealthy one percent have used their influence to directly or indirectly lower their taxes or reduce the chance that they might have to pay more down the line. To do this they have:

1. stopped the President and the Congress from increasing their tax rate to come closer in proportion to those who sweep out their offices.

2. attacked all unions directly and especially public service unions by forcing budget cuts and through media advertising falsehoods.

94

3. resisted health care reform in the legislature and through the media.

4. are trying to repeal those health care reforms that have already been enacted.

5. resisted extending unemployment insurance benefits.

6. closed public libraries or greatly reduced their services.

7. resisted government funded projects to improve our crumbling infrastructure.

8. are fighting to repeal government safety, health and welfare regulations.

9. fired teachers, aids and coaches as they worked to cut education programs.

10. closed many public schools.

11. fought environmental regulations.

12. tried to eliminate the EPA.

13. resisted attempts to resurrect the now successful American auto industry.

14. fomented legislation making voting difficult for minorities.

15. fought against attempts to bring manufacturing back to our shores.

16. resisted funding for public transportation.

17. proposed using child labor to clean schools.

18. trying to direct public opinion against food stamps; preferring that those down on their luck starve and die.

Their resistance to all this legislation, regulation and programs beneficial to the public is based on their belief that this will ultimately result in an increase in their tax obligation.

To justify this outrageous greed they use the argument that these programs and statutes will increase the national debt. They issue dire warnings that that our descendants will be burdened with a crushing debt that they will be unable to pay without the great loss of a rewarding life style.

What they fail to say, however, is that their conservative fiscal and environmental policies will force our descendants to be faced with:

1. a failing power grid.

2. an overloaded and inadequate sewer and storm drain system in many of our cities.

3. failing dikes and levies in low lying areas.

4. a lack of skilled labor due to poor schools.

5. a shrinking customer base due to few manufacturing jobs.

6. inadequate transportation due to poor roads, bridges and railroads.

7. poor public health due to inferior health care as well as polluted air and water.

8. A further shrinking of our domestic manufacturing capabilities due to an insufficient infrastructure to support large manufacturing installations.

The efforts of the filthy rich to maintain their unjustly low taxes by such obstructionist means would turn our country into a third world nation. But the national debt might be somewhat lower.

XII

The extreme right has frequently used the Constitutional guarantee of religious freedom to obfuscate their continued obstruction to any government action to promote the general welfare. The first and fourteenth amendments to the United States Constitution guarantees freedom of religion to all citizens. The amendments also imply a separation of church and state. This concept of separation has been upheld by the Supreme Court on several occasions.

At this time there is a large, generally liberal drive to create more fairness in the United States tax code. In an attempt to obscure the issue, conservatives have leaped on the opportunity to bring up the issue of religious freedom, accusing the left of denying this right to the Catholic Church.

This has come about because the administration decided that facilities owned and/or operated by the church must include full medical coverage for all their employees just as other establishments are compelled to do. This ruling did not include the church itself, but only non church operations such as schools and hospitals. This full coverage included birth control services and prescriptions.

The church complained that this was against their teachings and beliefs. They complained that they did not want to pay for this. They believe that providing these medical services is a sin. In order to settle the situation, the President compromised by insisting that the services be provided, but would be paid for by the health insurer. There would be no participation by the church owned facility in providing, managing or in any way being involved.

Conservative forces in Congress began a campaign to overturn the decision to cover women's health issues in America. A bill was introduced to allow any employer to deny any health coverage to employees for which the employer had a religious or moral objection. If passed, this bill would allow an employer to deny coverage for any reason. Imagine an employer who believes the population is growing too fast. Imagine this employer denying medical coverage for child birth and all related costs because it is against his belief in population control. Thankfully, the bill was defeated; but just barely.

This bill along with new controversy over the long resolved issue of birth control itself was fomented by the right to create a furore obscuring the debate over tax fairness. Their goal to use religious issues to drown out attempts to secure social justice for the electorate has achieved some success. All over the country women's rights are being questioned by conservatives on religious grounds. A leading conservative presidential candidate has expressed his feeling like, "throwing up", after reading President Kennedy's speech about his belief in the separation of church and state. This same candidate said in a speech that sixty percent of young people who attend university, lose their faith there. Of course, this was baseless nonsense. There are no statistics to support such a silly

99

contention. The controversy, however, has been successful in distracting the public's attention away from tax fairness allowing the filthy rich to amass more wealth than that of many nations.

In those states that are prohibiting equal medical care and imposing absurd quasi- medical procedures and restrictions for women based on dubious religious grounds are often justified by evoking the concept of state's rights.

Many times states enact laws that seem not to follow Constitutional standards. Before such laws can be challenged, and brought before the Supreme court for decision, local governments make a plea in the press trying to gain public support. They use a concept of, "state's rights" to justify their position.

Recently, several states have passed laws restricting women's access to health care and limiting their right to reproductive freedom. There are states putting up barriers to the voting rights of the poor, the disabled, the elderly as well as various minorities. These conservative state legislators and governors are doing this, they say, to prevent widespread voter fraud. However, serious voter fraud has not been an issue in our country. Why are conservative state legislators and governors taking steps to prevent a criminal behavior that does not exist? Is it just a coincidence that these disenfranchised groups tend to be liberal voters?

The concept of, "state's rights," seems to stem from the

100

belief that our country was originally a group of thirteen autonomous states that banded together forming a union to oppose Britain. In reality, however, they were never fully independent states. They were British Crown colonies governed by royal appointees and the English Parliament.

Four states of our union do not even referred to themselves as states, but rather commonwealths. These are the Commonwealth of Massachusetts, The Commonwealth of Virginia, The Commonwealth of Pennsylvania and later on The Commonwealth of Kentucky. Are these really states or are the other states really commonwealths? In any case none of them are or ever really were autonomous states in that although they had some authority within their borders they had no ability to deal with other nations except to protect themselves against incursions upon their territory before English troops could arrive to protect them.

The concept of separation of church and state has existed in America from the earliest days before the revolution. Roger Williams, the founder of *Rhode Island and Providence Plantations*, (Rhode Island), in the middle of the seventeenth century wrote at various times his belief in the separation of church and state. His beliefs in secular government appeared in several of his works including, *The Bloudy Tenent of Persecution for Cause of Conscience,* published in sixteen forty four.

The founder of the British Crown colony of Maryland, Lord Baltimore, caused the passing of the second law in British North

America guaranteeing religious freedom and the separation of church and state. Insuring freedom from Church of England rule, he fomented the passing of, *The Maryland Toleration Act*. Although this law was written to protect Christians of differing denominations from Church of England persecution, it was also applied to non-Christians as well. An example of this was the trial of a Jew named Jacob Lumbrozo in sixteen fifty eight. Mr. Lumbrozo was accused of saying that Jesus Christ was neither the son of God nor could he make miracles. The Maryland Toleration Act was written for the protection of Christians. Denying the holiness of Jesus Christ was still considered blasphemy and punishable by death. Nevertheless, saying that he was only answering a question, Jacob Lumbrozo was released and given full citizenship under the Maryland Toleration Act.

Our founding fathers held mostly to the same belief in a secular government. Thomas Jefferson held that belief. He wrote, *"every country and every age, the priest has been hostile to liberty. He is always in alliance with the despot...they have perverted the purest religion ever preached to man into mystery and jargon, unintelligible to all mankind, and therefore the safer for their purposes."*

It was not just at the time of the founding of our country that prominent Americans held a position in support of the separation of church and state. During his nineteen sixty election campaign President Kennedy said, *"I believe in an America where the separation of church and state is absolute—*

where no Catholic prelate would tell the President (should he be Catholic) how to act, and no Protestant minister would tell his parishioners for whom to vote—where no church or church school is granted any public funds or political preference—and where no man is denied public office merely because his religion differs from the President who might appoint him or the people who might elect him. I believe in an America that is officially neither Catholic, Protestant nor Jewish—where no public official either requests or accepts instructions on public policy from the Pope, the National Council of Churches or any other ecclesiastical source—where no religious body seeks to impose its will directly or indirectly upon the general populace or the public acts of its officials—and where religious liberty is so indivisible that an act against one church is treated as an act against all.

[...] I do not speak for my church on public matters—and the church does not speak for me. Whatever issue may come before me as President—on birth control, divorce, censorship, gambling or any other subject—I will make my decision in accordance with these views, in accordance with what my conscience tells me to be the national interest, and without regard to outside religious pressures or dictates. And no power or threat of punishment could cause me to decide otherwise. But if the time should ever come—and I do not concede any conflict to be even remotely possible—when my office would require me to either violate my conscience or violate the national interest, then I would resign the office; and I hope any conscientious public

servant would do the same."

In 1786, five years before the Bill of Rights, The Virginia Statute for Religious Freedom, written by Thomas Jefferson, was enacted.

In a letter of 1802, Mr. Jefferson wrote, "*Believing with you that religion is a matter which lies solely between man and his god, that he owes account to none other for his faith or his worship, that the legitimate powers of government reach actions only, and not opinions, I contemplate with sovereign reverence that act of the whole American people which declared that their "legislature" should "make no law respecting an establishment of religion, or prohibiting the free exercise thereof," thus building a wall of separation between church and State. Adhering to this expression of the supreme will of the nation in behalf of the rights of conscience, I shall see with sincere satisfaction the progress of those sentiments which tend to restore to man all his natural rights, convinced he has no natural right in opposition to his social duties.*"

James Madison, in support of Thomas Jefferson and the concept of separation of church and state, wrote, "*practical distinction between Religion and Civil Government is essential to the purity of both, and as guaranteed by the Constitution of the United States.*"

Even before The Bill of Rights was written, the original United States Constitution in article six, said, "*no religious Test shall ever be required as a Qualification to any Office or public Trust under the United States"*.

On more than one occasion, the Supreme Court has supported the views of President Jefferson. In eighteen seventy nine, the court maintained that Jefferson's opinions on the separation of church and state, *"may be accepted almost as an authoritative declaration of the scope and effect of the first amendment."*

XIII

It would seem that recent Supreme Court decisions have been detrimental to the national welfare. This perception is growing in many circles and the Occupy movement is beginning to demonstrate against the courts. What has the court done and why has it done it?

The Supreme Court was founded in our original Constitution as one of three branches constituting the U.S. Government. It is the sole arbiter of what is or is not allowed by our Constitution. It is that branch of government that protects our liberties and serves to protect us from excesses by our own government.

This recent ruling of the court in the Citizens United case is not the only unpopular decision that they have made. There have been others in the past. In eighteen fifty seven the court threw out the Missouri compromise which was an agreement that a slave that sets foot in a free state is free and no longer a slave. The court decided that no person of African ancestry could be an American citizen, and more importantly that he was the property of his owner and it was unconstitutional for any state to deprive the citizen of another state of his property.

The ruling that people of African ancestry could not be citizens is and was ludicrous. However, the ruling on the constitutionality of depriving a citizen of his or her property was a correct one for the Constitution as it existed at that time. What the court actually did was to point out a constitutional flaw that had to be corrected or amended. It took the bloodiest war in American history to bring about this constitutional correction known as the thirteenth amendment. This amendment prohibited any form of slavery, or bondage.

The Constitution, as originally written, was not the same document as today. It was written for an eighteenth century population with different mores, expectations, education, problems, fears, technology and economy.

Although written for Americans of the eighteenth century, it nevertheless had to be amended before the states would ratify it. These first ten amendments, referred to as the, "Bill of Rights", were enacted by Congress because of the widespread fear of the growth of an American monarchy. These original amendments were intended only as protection for white, land owning men. The extension of the Bill of Rights to apply to all citizens had to wait for further congressional and court actions in years to come.

The United States at the time of the adoption of the Constitution was primarily an agricultural nation. Slavery was common practice throughout the country. Women were second class citizens

In more recent times the Supreme Court has come to an unpopular decision about election law. During the Vietnam War many young people were being conscripted into the military at age eighteen. This produced an outcry from those of draft age complaining that they were old enough to be put in harm's way in the military, but could not vote to participate in the decision to be sent off to war.

President Nixon recognized this injustice and signed an extension of the nineteen sixty five voting rights act prohibiting states from denying the vote to those over eighteen years of age in all federal, state and local elections.

The law was challenged as being unconstitutional by the states of Oregon and Texas. They argued that neither the President nor congress had the authority to force states to raise the minimum voting age in state or local elections. The court agreed and the local provisions of the law were struck down. This created a complicated problem registering voters as there would have to be separate registrations for young voters in local versus national elections. This was especially a problem as both elections were often held at the same time. This decision pointed out a constitutional deficiency that was was soon corrected by the ratification of the twenty sixth amendment to the constitution which guaranteed the voting age to be no higher than eighteen years nationwide.

There were other instances where amendments to the constitution were deemed necessary and ratified by the states into law. Two such examples were amendments number nineteen which guaranteed women the right to vote and twenty four which struck down the use of a poll tax to bar citizens from voting. There are other amendments in place to correct constitutional inadequacies including our hallowed, "Bill of Rights".

The Supreme Court does not base its decisions on popularity, economics or anything other than their interpretation of constitutionality. Although their decisions are not cast in stone, it is rare when the court has reversed itself. But their decisions have, as been pointed out, resulted in popular actions to amend our constitution. The time has come once again for such action.

Recently, the President proposed a reduction in the highest tax rate from thirty five to twenty eight percent. Linked to this tax rate reduction for the wealthy one percent would be an elimination of loop holes and special interest deductions that they have enjoyed. The deductions and loop holes have been reducing their actual tax payments from the thirty five percent that they are supposed to pay, to what some estimate as more like thirteen to fourteen percent. When this proposal comes before Congress, I don't believe it has any chance for passage. I think that the conservative forces will do all that they can to defeat it. Would this really be in the public interest?

The purpose of the United States Congress is to satisfy the obligations of the preamble to the United Sates Constitution. Both houses of Congress are obligated to act in support of the general welfare and to insure domestic tranquility among other things. Is that really what they have been doing? Will that be what they are most likely to do when this tax bill goes to the capital?

As many have said over the years, the special interests

have taken over the United States Government. By making promises of huge monetary donations to political campaigns by paid lobbyists to elected officials, the voice of the general public is drowned out.

The filthy rich can influence government to do their bidding by making commitments of enormous financial support through lobbying. They can then satisfy these commitments through virtually unregulated political contributions to superpacs.

It has been shown here that the influence of big money on politics has often resulted in gross government inaction to the detriment of the population. This deleterious effect has resulted in the deterioration of our infrastructure, the erosion of our economy and great difficulties providing basic health services for our citizenry. These, as well as numerous other complications that have resulted from this unholy alliance of government and extreme wealth, have yet another ugly face.

There are many in our country that feel uncomfortable, some even fearful, about attending the theater, or going to the mall, or even sending their kids to school. These people are not afraid of disease or accident. They fear bloody mass murder. They fear murder by some lunatic with a military assault rifle having a thirty round magazine. This military weapon system can kill every time the trigger is pulled. The trigger can be pulled thirty times before the weapon must be reloaded. Reloading with thirty more cartridges takes just two or three seconds.

One or two people armed with an assault rifle like an AK47 or an M16 or the original German Sturmgewehr of World War Two can hold off many troops of an invading military force. These weapons, unlike a submachine gun, do not fire a pistol cartridge but rather a somewhat smaller version of a high powered rifle cartridge. This gives these rifles long range accuracy as well as extremely destructive striking force.

These weapons are short, light and designed for rapid fire.

111

This means that the recoil of one shot after another doesn't tend to jolt the barrel off its target. The great striking force of these rifles combined with long range and rapid fire accuracy makes them particularly deadly. Because of their light weight and because their ammunition is easy to carry in large quantities, they have become the ideal military small arms weapon. This is the purpose for which they were originally designed.

While the munitions manufacturers have been making fortunes selling assault rifles to the general public, they are somewhat different than military issue. The differences, however, are miniscule. The rifle issued to troops for combat have a switch that the soldier can use to select semi or fully automatic fire. A fully automatic weapon will fire continuously as long as the trigger is held down. It will continue firing until it runs out of ammunition. A semi automatic firearm will shoot every time the trigger is pulled as fast as the shooter can pull it. The civilian version has no fully automatic fire option. They are sold as semi automatic rifles with the selector switch eliminated.

This difference between the military and civilian versions of the weapon does not negate the disastrous effect of assault rifles on life in our country. For many of the assault rifle models that are in civilian hands, conversion to fully automatic operation is a simple matter. The parts and procedures for such a conversion are readily available on the internet.

Even as a semi automatic rifle, the assault weapon's military design means that it far outclasses any sort of pistol that would be carried by any police officer or armed guard. Because these guns can use twenty, thirty or even one hundred round drum magazines they are ideal for killing large numbers of people in short order. They are devices made for human slaughter!

This class of firearm can be used for hunting or target shooting or for personal and home defense. This is, however, not what they were designed for. A purpose built target rifle is far more accurate. Target rifles are equipped with a target stock, target sights, a superior trigger designed for target use and will shoot circles around a military rifle at shooting competitions. Because target shooters are not faced with hundreds of hostile targets attacking them, high capacity detachable magazines are neither necessary nor desirable on the target range. Rifles designed for target shooting are usually bolt action or even single shot firearms. For these reasons assault rifle target competitions pit assault rifles against other assault rifles as they cannot compete against real target rifles.

It would seem that an assault rifle is an effective home defense weapon. It is. Other firearms that can be used for hunting can also be effective home defense weapons. Actually, a shotgun that only holds two shells would be much more effective for this purpose. A person's home is not going to be assaulted

113

by hoards of violent criminals at the same time. A weapon that can unleash a firestorm of bullets is hardly necessary against one or two intruders trying to break in. Hitting the target is more important than the number of bullets than can be fired. Hitting a target at close range with a shotgun is much more likely.

Hunting rifles have been used for centuries to put meat on the table. They have been designed to match the game they were to be used to shoot. A squirrel rifle would be useless against an elephant or bison. A buffalo or elephant gun would blow a squirrel or rabbit to bits, leaving little or no meat for the hunter.   They are also designed to match the terrain in which they are to be used. A deer hunter in the dense Pennsylvania forest would probably choose a short barrel rifle firing a heavy, relatively slow moving bullet. In this type of hunting, in heavy brush, there is little opportunity for long range shots. Here, the heavy bullet is much less likely to be deflected by a twig or tree branch as would a light, high velocity, long range round. The American military style assault rifle fires such a round. Essentially it uses a twenty two caliber high velocity cartridge, which is not particularly suitable for deer hunting in the eastern United States.

In the western U.S. the hunting is different. Here long range shots at large game is common. Instead of the dense woods of the East, there are open plains with large herds of grazing animals. Game is frequently three or four hundred yards away or even further. This is the land of the high velocity, heavy bullet.

It would seem that this is where the assault rifle can be used as an affective hunting tool. However, it has been designed to kill a one hundred fifty pound person at up to three hundred yards distant; not a fifteen hundred pound bison at three hundred or more yards away. Assault rifles can unleash a hail of bullets at a game animal. However, hunters seek a clean, one shot kill. A hail of bullets is neither sporting, nor effective nor does it leave much meat for the table. Although an assault rifle can be used for hunting, it clearly was not designed for this purpose and is actually not well suited for it.

Many hunting rifles are beautifully made. Some have stocks of highly figured walnut or tiger maple or other magnificent and exotic wood. Usually hand carved, and hand fitted to the precisely made and finely polished barrel and action. Hunting rifles are often a source of pride to the owner and are handed down to their heirs.

In contrast to the wood and fine polished steel of the prized hunting rifle, the combat assault rifle is designed for cheap mass production as well as battlefield effectiveness. It is made of aluminum, cheap sheet metal stampings, and plastic. They are simply ugly. One would think that these weapons are inexpensive. However, that is not the case. A civilian version of the US M16, purchased at a gun store can cost two thousand dollars or more.

Because of their limited usefulness, unattractive appearance, and high price, it is reasonable to assume that only a very few people own them. In fact, they are among the most popular firearms on the market. This is one of the reasons for their enormously high price.

The reason for such high volume sales seems to be that many gun owners are defending themselves against a military invasion. The invasion that they have been arming themselves against is one they believe will come from The United States Government. Their fear is that the government will disarm them and everyone else by force in order to establish some sort of totalitarian state.

This belief causes large numbers of people to fearfully reject any sort of firearm licensing, restriction or regulation. Their fear in this case is that the government will then have records of everyone with a gun and will be able to confiscate everyone's firearms.

The feared government attack on gun owners is thought by many to start with an eroding of our second amendment constitutional rights. By limiting people's access to military style rifles; by limiting public access to automatic pistols and revolvers through local licensing requirements and by requiring background checks on all firearms sales; some in the gun owning public fear this as the first step in tracking down and arresting all gun owners. They, therefore, cling to the second amendment as the potential salvation of our country.

This fear of privately owned firearms being confiscated by the federal government has prevented any sort of reasonable legislation from being enacted. Many gun owners have been following the National Rifle Association's policies and activities to resist regulations that would assure that firearms are restricted to citizens of good standing and emotional stability as well as restricting the sale of military style weapons.

The fact that we live in a free society is credited by many to the second amendment of the United States Constitution. However, the second amendment is not at all clear. This amendment protects our right to bear arms in the context of keeping a militia. The amendment states, "A well regulated Militia, being necessary to the security of a free State, the right of the people to keep and bear Arms, shall not be infringed." Appearing simple and readily understandable, it is only under a more careful review that problems begin to show up.

The greatest problem with the second amendment is similar to the problem we have had with other parts of our Constitution. Our national document was written in the eighteenth century. It is the age of this document and the second amendment that presents problems on several levels.

The first problem is one of language. The English language has changed considerably in the last two hundred plus years. The definitions and connotations of many words, as well as the use of language has changed considerably. Even the use of individual letters have changed as with the letter, "S", written in the eighteenth century in the form of the modern letter, "F".

What is meant by the eighteenth century term, "militia", or the eighteenth century concept of a "well regulated militia" is not all all clear. What is generally accepted is that both the general population of those times and the governments of the individual states were concerned that a strong central government might turn into a totalitarian state or a monarchy as earlier under the English. Before the new Constitution would be ratified, safeguards were insisted upon to prevent this occurrence. Because there wasn't a standing army to protect against invasion or to insure peoples' personal rights and liberties it was felt important to have the ability to call up a military force that would be immediately available for action.

With an armed and ready civilian population, it was felt that our country could be defended from both domestic and foreign threats. Soldiers in the seventeen hundreds were armed with edged weapons, (swords, etc.), artillery, muskets, pistols and rifles. Our civilian population was generally untrained in dueling or combat with swords. Then, as now, no one would have an artillery piece in their possession; but for personal protection and to put food on the table, most folks then had a rifle or musket. Most eighteenth century citizens were familiar with firearms. Many were dependent on their rifles to put food on their tables and were quite skilled with them.

If there were to be some emergency, a militia of civilians

armed with their personal weapons could present an effective force to defend the land. This was demonstrated by the Minute Men during the revolution. This was the reason that a second amendment had to be included in the Constitution.

An attacking force today would have weapons that no militia armed with small arms could put up any sort of serious defense against. Today we have a standing military which is the largest on earth to defend us. They have been defending us magnificently ever since The War of Eighteen Twelve.

A militia armed with civilian weapons would not be able to defend the country against any threat other than an imaginary one. Nevertheless, there are many groups that have formed into organizations that consider themselves to be militias. These people are arming themselves with military style assault rifles and are training to be ready for the federal government attacks that they fear are soon to begin.

It is these people who are at the forefront of military weapon sales and resistance to any restriction upon them. Why is it that they feel this way?

Despite the attention in the media garnered by the horror of the mass murders committed with assault rifles, those weapons are not the most serious firearm problem that we have.

By far our biggest gun violence problem is with handguns. Handgun crimes, injuries, murders and suicides far outstrip those committed by shoulder weapons. Some statistics show handgun deaths to be close to ten times the number of those caused by long arms. The concealable nature of handguns makes them the perfect tool for committing robberies and murders. They seem to fill the bill for gang violence as well.

More the scourge of inner city life than in rural areas, cities and counties have tried to pass legislation to control gun violence. Mostly these attempts have failed. Many local bills have been struck down as being in violation of the second amendment. Those that have been upheld have been only marginally successful as handguns are being brought into communities where they are illegal in wholesale numbers. It has been clear for many years that legislation at the federal level is the only real curb on this horror. Federal legislation to control the firearms industry in the United States has been successfully fought for years.

Groups of gun lobbyists have fought tooth and nail to prevent any restriction on the sale of handguns, assault rifles or any other type of weapon. Those same groups have been agitating against any sort of licensing to own a gun as well as being loudly against any sort of background check prior to selling a gun.

Just to stop and think about this for a moment, a person cannot add a sink to his bathroom, or a light fixture to her hallway, or even catch a fish without a proper license. Yet any talk of licensing gun owners is met with a furor of controversy. At this time in South Africa a man is on trial for shooting his girlfriend by mistake through a closed door. Had there been some sort of training in firearm handling in order to obtain a license, could that death have been avoided? Is this terror of any sort of gun regulation rational? Where does it come from?

What is the source of the bone chilling fear that seems to have the gun owning public so terrified of our own government? How is it, that any discussion of gun regulation is interpreted as the precursor to an American dictatorship?

There must be some sort of organization that has the means as well as the reason to whip up such a furor. The National Rifle Association, (NRA), is just such an organization.

Ostensibly formed to serve gun collectors, shooters and hunters, the NRA through it's member services and The American Rifleman magazine has been the firearm owning public's technical and political guide. Through the years the organization has been the authority on gun history, gun design, gun collecting and ballistics. They have continuously served the political interests of the gun owning public through numerous magazine articles as well as public support for candidates and political positions on gun related topics. Their lobbying and financial support for gun friendly candidates have been very successful over the years. In every issue they run a column called, "The Armed Citizen", in which they publicize a news story in which a crime is prevented through the actions of a citizen with a personally owned firearm.

Nevertheless, in spite of their position that all responsible citizens should own a weapon, they have been

121

reasonable in their arguments. This is illustrated by the historic NRA point of view that although the public's right to own a gun should not be infringed, all those buying a gun should be subjected to a thorough criminal background check as well as checking their personal history for mental or emotional difficulties.

This no longer seems to be the case. The latest opinion expressed by CEO and Executive Vice President Wayne La Pierre is a complete rejection of any sort of vetting of firearms buyers. They also reject any restriction on magazine size, or the sale of virtually any weapon including assault rifles, and it would seem mortars and heavy machine guns as well as field artillery.

Despite these unrealistic positions of the NRA leadership, the general membership does not seem to share them as polls show their increasing support for comprehensive background checks for gun purchasers. As of this writing the general public also seems to overwhelmingly support a system of thorough background checks for all firearm purchases. What in our country has changed to cause this organization to shift views? Even to adopt a position that their own membership does not really support?

There is, however, method to their madness. A connection seems to exist between the NRA and the firearms and ammunition manufacturers. Back during the time that Charlton Heston was the spokesman for the NRA they publicly voiced their support for the weapons industry. At the present time there are gun manufacturer executives on the board of directors of the NRA. It is very much in the interest of the firearm makers that there be no legislation passed that will have a negative affect on sales.

In order for the munitions manufacturers to act in support of their own interests, they make huge monetary political contributions, through the NRA. The NRA, by means of funding from the arms industry is actively waging political war against any and all candidates that propose anything that might have the slightest deleterious effect on gun or ammunition sales. Because sales figures are hardly a viable political cause, they had to find one that would be.

Not only did they find an issue, they found one that in itself would stimulate sales into a fever pitch. What would cause such a run on the arms market that it has even become difficult, nation wide, to find ammunition in all calibers?

The NRA for years has stressed the second amendment words that, "the right of the people to keep and bear Arms, shall not be infringed." Those words are not the words of the entire amendment which clearly states that this is in the context of keeping an armed militia.

Besides the fact that a militia is unnecessary today, the very concept of firearms is completely different. A criminal or mentally ill person today could arm himself with an assault rifle or automatic pistol and shoot so many people before he could be stopped that he would be committing a one person massacre. Such weapons were unknown in the eighteenth century when the second amendment was written. There is no evidence that

brilliant minds like those of President Jefferson or Dr,.
Franklin or anyone else anywhere, ever wrote a word intimating
they had even fantasized about such a thing.

A personal firearm in the eighteenth century would be
either a flintlock musket or a flintlock rifle or a flintlock
pistol. The flintlock musket was the rapid fire weapon of the
day. Because the barrel was smooth inside, *(smooth bore)*,and as
all firearms had to be loaded from the front, *(muzzle loaded)*,
the bullet could be slid down the length of the musket barrel
easily and relatively quickly.

To load and fire a musket one had to swab out the barrel
with a cloth patch and ram rod in order to clear out any burning
material from the previous shot. Then pull the hammer back to
half cock position. Next obtain a paper cartridge containing
powder and ball. Bite a hole in the end of the cartridge
permitting a small amount of powder to be poured into the pan.
Then the rest of the powder is poured down the barrel followed
by ramming the paper cartridge wrapped ball all the way down the
barrel with the rod. Return the rod to it's holder in the
musket, pull the hammer back to full cock. Now the weapon is
ready to fire with the pull of the trigger. The procedure for a
flintlock pistol was much the same.

Nowhere in the procedure is there an instruction to aim.
One would point a smooth bore weapon in the general direction of
your target, but aim, no. These weapons didn't even have sights
with which to aim them. The reason for this is the poor accuracy

124

of the smooth bore musket. Actually, poor accuracy is a gross under statement. There was very little chance for a musketeer to hit anything. Muskets were used by eighteenth century armies in mass volley fire. Accuracy was not important or even considered, rapid mass fire was.

In the old world most all woodland was owned by the aristocracy for their own private purposes and proscribed from public use. However, the abundance of open woodland allowed the general public to hunt for food to feed his family in the Americas without any real restrictions.

With the inaccurate musket as the available weapon for hunting, success was often marginal. The solution to this was being produced by the German gunsmiths that had settled in Pennsylvania. They employed the old world discovery that a set of spiral groves on the inside of a gun barrel would impart a spin to the bullet causing a dramatic improvement in accuracy. Called long rifles because of the weapon's enormous size and because the German word for the grooves in the barrel is rifling. They were often called Kentucky Long Rifles because they were widely favored by frontier trappers and hunters in Kentucky.

During the Revolution the British, to their grief. learned of the effectiveness of the Kentucky Long Rifle. General Washington, for the first time in warfare, formed companies of riflemen. He used them to pick off British officers. The first ever use of snipers in warfare.

125

In spite of the accuracy and long range effectiveness of rifles, the musket remained the military's main weapon both here and in Europe until the outbreak of the Civil War. This was because it took even longer to load a rifle than a musket. The procedure to load a flintlock rifle was essentially the same as that of the musket with one real difference. In order to impart significant spin to the ball, the rifling must be able to grab it. Therefore, when loading, the ball must be forced down the barrel with the rifling grooves actually cutting into the ball which was wrapped in a cloth patch. A deranged criminal of the time would have been able to create more mayhem and terror with an edged weapon than a firearm.

Those who support the NRA's position and in so doing, the munitions manufacturers, are giving an almost religious zeal of support to an amendment concerning eighteenth century life in this, the twenty first century.

As of this writing, The United States Senate may debate a national requirement for universal background checks for all gun purchases. The reason that the debate might or might not take place is that thirteen conservative senators have stated their intention to filibuster the issue in order to prevent the debate. They have stated that they might do this in defense of the second, very obsolete, amendment. In the face of eighty five percent public support for firearms control and regulation, our government is and has done less than nothing. Both federal and state legislation has hindered sane gun regulation by limiting manufacturer's liability for murder and suicide as well as restricting the passage of any legal controls.

Would there be such a fear of government gun confiscation and the coming federal dictatorship which never seems to arrive, without the funding and support of the manufacturers who are profiting by the fear they create. It was President Eisenhower who coined the phrase while he warned us to beware the, "military/industrial complex". I don't think that he thought the, "complex", would drag us into a shooting war against our own babies.

Does it seem likely that without private campaign contributions, there would be such political resistance to any kind of firearms control. With an overwhelming public support for universal background checks how could those senators have the nerve to even think of preventing a public debate on the issue. They do these things and talk of what the American people want! They who have sold our democracy to the highest bidder!

To date there is no supporting evidence that the Iraq invasion was trumped up to generate business for the arms manufacturing industry. There is no evidence that it wasn't either. It is odd though that the taxes for wealthy industrialists were lowered and all the money to pay these industrialists for the weapons they were asked to make was borrowed by the administration. If there were no private political contributions would this question even arise?

The Occupy Wall Street movement has acted against the privileged one percent by demonstrating against the big banks, big wall street investment groups, big insurance companies as well as filthy rich individuals. Recently they have begun to demonstrate against the Supreme Court. Their actions have come from the onerous Citizens United decision. They have also started demonstrating against Congress for its lack of action in support of the general welfare. They have been somewhat successful by affecting public perceptions of big business and union busting policies.

They have acted together with others to force the major banks to roll back many of their outrageous ATM fees. They have fomented action against unconscionable foreclosure practices with state as well as federal investigations of bank behavior. Their publicity has caused government action to start forcing the big banks to begin to offer monetary compensation to their victims. The Occupy movement has created a public desire to close accounts in big national banks and open them in smaller, local banks and credit unions.

The time is ripe for the Occupy movement to focus its power to initiate real change in America. It is time to reform American election law. The recent Supreme Court decisions have pointed the way. The Court has highlighted constitutional weaknesses that must be corrected.

The object of constitutional reform must be to reduce the

influence of extremely wealthy and powerful special interests upon the policies and actions of the government. This change should be to separate big money from federal elections and by doing so, reduce the power of special interest lobbyists. There are several ways to achieve this while still keeping public interest and participation in government and politics.

Government officials are elected to govern for their full term. Yet, when incumbents are approaching re-election they spend considerably more time electioneering than governing.

It seems only reasonable for this to happen, but for how long must it go on? How much time is needed for politicians to voice their positions on the policies they wish to extol. Is a month too little time to have a TV debate, several speeches, a few interviews and, perhaps, a late night appearance with David Letterman or Jon Stuart? Hopefully, given even more time, they should be able to present their case to the public. After perhaps two months, the public could make a thoughtful decision.

This is, of course, not what is happening. Politicians are often electioneering for a year or more. The result of this is that the voting public is subjected to an onslaught of phone calls, junk mail, and an endless tirade of negative ads. These negative advertisements are often half truths, distortions, or sometimes outright lies. All this activity, for this length of time, requires huge amounts of money. To obtain the enormous war chest needed to run such a campaign candidates must spend a disproportionate amount of time fund raising.

129

If, however, a candidate or proponent advocating a referendum, could obtain all or most of the funding needed to run a lengthy campaign from one extremely rich donor, more time can be spent electioneering. Garnering support from the very wealthy becomes a strategy for victory. But, the most significance part of this process, is the control over political candidates and parties exercised by extremely wealthy donors.

If, through constitutional amendment, the time spent electioneering were limited by law and the funding required to run political campaigns substantially reduced, there would be noticeably less influence from the extraordinarily rich. Also reduced would be the time available to dredge up dirt from the opposition's past. This would reduce not only the time available for negative political advertising but also the time available to get facts supporting political negativity.

Candidates running for public office under such legislation would have to spend electioneering time stressing their qualifications for holding office as well as their ideas and plans for government. Time limitations would allow only a minimum amount of mud slinging. This should result in cleaner elections, a less disgusted, more informed and more involved public, and most importantly, a great reduction in the influence of money on politics.

Such changes to our election processes would have to be accomplished through radical Constitutional amendment. Can our government, our tradition of personal liberty and our system of free elections remain viable with such a drastic constitutional

overhaul? Is there precedence for such a significant

governmental change in our national history?

XVI

During the year 1764 the east coast of North America was occupied by thirteen British Crown colonies. These colonies had colonial assemblies and other legislative bodies that governed their internal affairs along with governors appointed by the Crown. The colonies had demographics that were different, one from another. Some relied on fishing and whaling for products to market, others gathered, processed, and sold forest products. Most, however, were agricultural economies. These agricultural colonies, however, mostly grew different crops on differing soils, in different climates. The American colonies were considered to be English. Yet some, like Pennsylvania, had a large German population and New York had a large Dutch population to name just two. Although they had a certain degree of autonomy, they were, nevertheless, British subjects and followed the king's rule, as well as the laws passed by Parliament in London.

Besides the British, France also had a great interest and investment in North America. This eventually led to conflict. Native American tribes allied with French military units began attacking English settlements. To defend their colonies, the English also sent troops which resulted in what we now call the French and Indian war. The combined war effort of the colonists and the Royal Army were successful and the colonies remained English and at peace.

Across the ocean, however, things were not very peaceful in

Parliament. The royal coffers were depleted and the kingdom was heavily in debt because of the cost of defending the colonies during the recent war. Therefore, Parliament felt that the American Colonies, whom they had just defended, should begin to bear the cost of their own defense. They, therefore, passed laws that levied various taxes upon the American Colonists.

Because these British colonies had no voice in their Parliament, nor any say about the taxes that they were going to have to pay, the new taxes were received in the colonies with outrage. There were demonstrations and riots as well as threats against royal tax collectors by organizations in the various colonies that called themselves, *The Sons of Liberty*. This resulted in mass resignations of most of the king's tax collectors. By hook or crook the colonists mostly succeeded in foiling the collection of the king's tax.

The outrage then shifted to London where both Parliament and King George were furious over the recalcitrance of the North Americans. In order to secure the tax funding they felt they needed from America, as well as a strong desire to teach their colonial subjects a lesson about obeying their monarch, the Stamp Act was passed. This taxed virtually all legal documents and printed periodicals as well as many other commodities. To enforce the collection of taxes an edict was passed that required the colonists to quarter British troops and supply them as well. Designed to quell resistance to British authority and taxation, these measures failed utterly.

In seventeen sixty six Parliament repealed the onerous
Stamp Act. But Parliament then enacted the Declaratory Act which
essentially said that Parliament could do anything they wanted
to do in their North American colonies, including any and all
taxation.

British-North American relations would worsen as new taxes
and edicts were imposed. Colonists responded with boycotts of
British goods as well as demonstrations and what ever forms of
resistance they could muster; even armed conflict in New York
over the cost of provisioning the royal troops that they had to
quarter.

Eventually the tax would be repealed. The locals responded
by lifting their boycotts and relations improved. Somehow,
however, relations never improved enough. New taxes and edicts
were forthcoming and the colonists responded with more costly
boycotts and other forms of resistance, especially against being
taxed without representation in Parliament. Tensions continued
to grow fomenting actions in response from the American
population.

In seventeen seventy two, through the urgings of Samuel
Adams and others, a town meeting in Boston created, *"Committees
of Correspondence,"* to coordinate Massachusetts' efforts to
resist the action of the Crown with the other colonies. The
coordinating colonies were now working together in a dawning
sense of unity.

Parliament continued to try to pass one tax after another

without allowing any colonial representation. Protests were met by Parliamentary actions designed to punish the colonies rather than generate revenue. All of these laws and edicts began to be called, *"The Intolerable Acts,"* by Americans throughout all the colonies. Finally, the *Committees of Correspondence* began calling for a meeting of representatives from all the colonies in order to decide on a uniform course of action that they could take vis a vis the policies of Parliament and the Crown. This was the first time that these British colonies began to function in a coordinated way.

Each of the colonies began a process of selecting representatives to be sent to Philadelphia where the meeting was to be held on September Fifth, Seventeen Seventy Four. Representatives from all the colonies save Georgia were eventually in attendance.

Now for the first time there were colonists referring to themselves as an American nation as well as a confederation of autonomous colonies. It was as a nation, in that seventeen seventy four meeting, that that they tried to propose a peaceful settlement with King George and Parliament. This representative group that was meeting in Philadelphia came to be known as, *"The Continental Congress"*, in order to differentiate it from local meetings that were called congresses that had been taking place within the several colonies. The colonials, finding themselves trying to deal with England in concert with the other colonies saw themselves as nation states operating in a confederation of nation states as well as British Crown colonies. They referred to their own meeting as, *"The United States of America in Congress Assembled"*. By sometimes looking at themselves as an assembly of sovereign nations, *(or states),* working together to solve a common problem, they were taking the first step towards independence from Great Britain.

Acting in concert made this first *Continental Congress* the first government of a new quasi nation. The fifty six representatives had a petition drawn up, signed and sent to King George asking for some redress from the Intolerable Acts. When this failed, Congress then put a severe boycott of all British trade across all the colonies. They established a system of boycott enforcement and obtained support from all necessary colonial assemblies. Another important accomplishment of the first Continental Congress was their decision to meet again in a year if the situation did not improve.

Clearly the situation in May of seventeen seventy five had not improved. Things had gotten worse as the first battles of the revolution had already begun in Lexington and Concord. John Hancock was picked as the President of this, the *Second Continental Congress*.

The *Second Continental Congress*, using the authority they had assumed for themselves at their first meeting the previous year, began to function for all intents and purposes as the government of a nation. In May of seventeen seventy six Congress required member colonies to draft their own separate constitutions and begin to govern themselves as full and independent nations. This lead to the drafting of the *Declaration of Independence* and formal separation from Britain.

John Adams argued successfully that Congress should declare the local armed resistance to British authority in Massachusetts, to be considered The Continental Army. At Mr. Adams' urging, they appointed George Washington as general. In addition they appointed a committee to draw up military rules and procedures for their new army and it's general.

To pay for the army, Congress prepared bills of credit that the various colonies agreed to repay. Congress ordered four armed vessels to be built and created a continental navy with Esek Hopkins as commodore.

Again acting as a functioning government, Congress initiated treaties with Indian tribes and began dialogues with foreign nations seeking their aid in the war against Great Britain.

The delegates to the *Second Continental Congress* also sought to legitimize their decisions and actions by drafting a legal document that would establish a continental governing body and rule of law. Thinking themselves having become a confederation of thirteen independent and sovereign nations working in concert or confederation they called their document, *"The Articles of Confederation"*. Because Congress was in session during the progress of the war; and the strife that lead to the conflict was fresh in the Congressional consciousness, the articles were written to prevent similar strife in the future. They were careful to prevent any centralized governmental power that they thought could become dictatorial in exercise of authority as they felt King George had done.

As Dr. Benjamin Franklin observed, "If we don't hang together, then we shall surely hang separately". Each of the thirteen now independent nation/states seems to have realized that they must work together to gain their freedom from Britain. The absence of a central governing authority was not only unnecessary in their unified struggle, it did not really apply to a community of sovereign nations.

When the war ended The United States of America was a group of thirteen associated but independent countries. Congress which by now was called the *Congress of the Confederation* had been given responsibility by the *Articles of Confederation* but little or no powers to enforce it's decisions or policies. With the war raging these deficiencies were not apparent as mostly all activity was devoted to the combined war effort. Now, however, these weaknesses began to present difficulties in the peaceful conduct of daily activity.

Chief among the new country's difficulties was the mind set of all strata of society. Those living in the United States did not consider themselves citizens of the United States. There actually was no such country. There was an American confederation of free and autonomous nations. A resident of any one of the states felt himself to be a citizen of that state.

138

People living in Connecticut, for example, would think of those in New York or Massachusetts as foreigners. Decisions that affected New Jersey would be looked upon by Pennsylvanians back then, as a decision affecting Argentina would be considered today, ie a foreign internal matter.

Although prohibited by the *Articles of Confederation*, states began to issue their own currencies which often became worthless. Interstate commerce began to be impeded by cross border tariffs and other impediments. Personal freedoms varied from state to state as did virtually all laws. Border disputes between the states was common and sometimes resulted in cross border military action. That this was prohibited by the *Articles of Confederation* had little or no affect as Congress had little or no power.

The United States of America was heavily in debt to France and Spain as well as other countries and individuals. The debts could not be satisfied because although charged with responsibility to pay, Congress had no authority to collect taxes and therefore had no funds in the treasury to pay with. Funds to pay debts and for any other purpose could only be requested from the States who were not enthusiastic about paying their share of war debts to Congress. With huge unsatisfied debts to other countries, international relations and trade began to suffer as it was clear that the U.S. had no means to pay its obligations.

Police and military force can only exist where there is an

139

economic resource to provide it. Since there was no economic power in Congress, there was no money to pay for any military to enforce congressional policy. If a military threat was perceived by any state, there was no central government to react to this. People in other states would consider this to be a foreign problem and neither their concern nor responsibility.

August 29, 1786 a faction of disenchanted revolutionary war veterans in Massachusetts began to protest about their economic plight with the post war depression and problems with worthless currency. Started by the war veteran, Daniel Shays, the rebels' first action was to close the Massachusetts courts. Things finally escalated into actual war. Called, *Shays Rebellion* the state was terrorized by the rebels. Because Congress could call up no troops without money, the rebellion was finally put down by the Massachusetts' state militia. *Shays Rebellion* made the inadequacies of the *Articles of Confederation* apparent to legislators and officials across the U.S.

Because Congress was essentially powerless, other nations began to take advantage of this. England had agreed at war's end to vacate all of their fortifications in the U.S., but remained in occupation of these forts because we could do nothing about it. France began to exclude us from using the Mississippi as a navigable waterway. This resulted in a French monopoly in shipping and passenger service up and down the Mississippi and we were shut out of this lucrative business. We had problems with the Spanish in Florida as well.

140

During the Revolution, Congress, the military, as well as the civilian population began to rally around George Washington. In the civil war the country rallied around Abraham Lincoln. During the Great Depression and World War II the country rallied around President Franklin Roosevelt. However, under the Articles of Confederation there was no one for the country to look to for leadership.

Because we were a confederation not really a country, we had no leader. There was a President of the Congress, but the President could serve only one year out of three and was only there to preside over congressional proceedings. The President had no real power and was elected by congressional delegates only. It is doubtful that the public even knew who he was or cared. Governance was a matter for the thirteen individual states, not congress.

Congressional activity was rapidly growing irrelevant. So much so that there were sometimes problems gathering a quorum and therefore times when congress could not meet. The public generally neither knew nor cared as government came from their separate state capitols. The difficulties and inability of Congress to function began to call attention for change.

Finally on May 25, 1787 the pressures for change finally resulted in a Constitutional Convention. After debate and discussion it was decided by the delegates that amending the Articles did not seem as though it would work. It was felt that the government should be redrawn from the ground up. Drawing from the writings of European philosophers and ideas they got from the organization of the Iroquois Nation as well as features gleaned from some of the various state legislatures they decided on a government with three major branches.

A legislative division or branch with two houses. One, the Senate with two senators representing each state and the other, The House of Representatives, having representation according to each state's population. This body comprised of two houses would be called, *The Congress of the United States of America*. It would be the duty of Congress to write and pass laws that would be in force across all the states.

For the first time there would be an elected leader. This person would serve as the executive branch of the government and would be an elected official with title of, *President of the United States of America*. It would be the President that would have the authority and governmental power to enforce the laws of Congress. The President would also act as Commander in Chief of all the now mostly unified country's military forces. The President would also have the responsibility to enforce the decisions of the third branch of government, the judiciary.

Congress can pass no law; nor can the President take any action that is prohibited by any of the articles of the United States Constitution. Preventing these occurrences would be the function of the judiciary headed by the Supreme Court. It would be the function of the court to determine the constitutionality of any congressional or presidential action. The court also can override state and local court decisions as well as gubernatorial actions that it deems unconstitutional.

This scrapping of the American confederacy and the articles governing it was not easy for the public to accept. The popular distrust of centralized authority as well as power, especially the power of taxation, was too close to the British authority that they had just defeated. It was also difficult for the states to surrender their governmental and financial power as well.

This can be illustrated by the reluctance of states to ratify the new constitution. Still fresh in the American mind was the trampling on what the people considered to be their rights as Englishmen and their rights now as New Yorkers, Virginians or Georgians, etc. To this end the new Constitution had to be amended before it could be ratified into law. These ten amendments, which we now call the Bill of Rights is considered by many as the most important part of our constitutional government.

Even after the ratification of the Constitution and the inauguration of President Washington, there were many who would not accept federal authority and felt that their freedom as citizens of their respective states was being abridged.

These feelings and public sentiments of the time are known to us through the historical record of various incidents that had occurred. One of the most important was the, *"Whiskey Rebellion"*.

The western counties of Pennsylvania in seventeen ninety four was largely agricultural and heavily involved in the growing of grain and the distillation of whiskey. The federal government in the then capital of Philadelphia decided to enforce the levy of an excise tax on distilled spirits. This was met by open hostility by the farmers and distillers. They began to rough up tax collectors and fomented riots in Pittsburg and elsewhere.

To deal with this problem and it's test of new federal authority, the President nationalized states' militias and sent fourteen thousand troops into western Pennsylvania to put down the insurrection. The show of force succeeded without firing a shot. Eventually Americans became used to federal authority and the force of the Constitution. Nevertheless, the power of the separate states was still very strong.

As time progressed the southern states and northern states developed differently. In the North the economy was based on manufacturing, fishing, shipping and small farms.

The south, however, developed large farms called plantations. Involved mainly in the production of rice, tobacco and most economically important, cotton. To be profitable the southern plantations needed huge labor forces to cultivate their crops. In order to maximize profits they used black slave labor. It was available, cheap and legal.

Bondage in the southern states was considered normal. Their slaves were thought to be an inferior type of humanity that

144

actually needed the guidance and structure provided by their owners. Also, their economy was totally dependent on slave labor.

Religious and moral outrage about southern slavery grew in the North culminating in the election of President Lincoln. Upon his election the southern states seceded from the union and formed their own government, *"The Confederate States of America"*. The bloodiest war in American history ensued.

Both the U.S. and the Confederacy held states' rights to be of paramount importance. Both militaries organized their forces state by state. Although there were military units that were raised by the federal government of both the U.S. and the C.S. The majority were raised by the states. Units were identified by the states that they came from. For example, the Second Battery Connecticut Light Artillery, or Fourteenth Illinois Infantry Regiment and so forth. It was common for soldiers who came from the same communities or even the same families to serve together and sometimes die together. This meant that whole families or sometimes nearly all the men from a community would be wiped out.

This state by state military organization was never repeated. After the Civil War, it became the federal government that began to raise, train and equip our military. For the first time our country was becoming mostly unified. With the death of the C.S.A. the American confederation of associated sovereign states became one unified country. Although states' rights is still sometimes an issue in modern politics, it is the federal government in which political and economic power reside.

When the Civil War ended and the country became more unified, the political, economic and military power of our country began to grow. We eventually grew into a world power along with other industrialized, unified nations. It is time now to take the next step to truly modernize our country.

The United States of America is the first modern democracy in the world. It is our country that lead the way to modern government. We were the nation that rejected the concept of rule by right of birth. We achieved this by working through a succession of upheavals and cataclysms. After each one the country grew stronger and life for our citizens became better.

We won our freedom from the English monarchy. The world expected our social experiment to fail and it almost did. The upheaval of separation from the mother country affected every aspect of life and commerce. There were many difficulties in conducting business and daily life in the United States confederation. Yet, at first, we prospered. However, our existence as an assembly of associated, sovereign states began to fail as the monarchies of Europe had predicted.

Another upheaval had to be endured. Despite our public distrust of central governmental power, we had to unify under a common flag, surrendering our multi- nation existence.

With adoption of the Constitution a person was no longer a citizen of an American state. There no longer was such a

146

citizenship. That person could only be a resident of a state. The person did, of course, become a citizen of the United States as a whole. That this was not the public mind set of the times can be gleaned from this remark of President Washington, *"We have now a national character to establish"*.

Tariffs, taxes and duties that were collected at state borders were no longer collectable. Federal taxes and other levies had to be sometimes collected by force. The authority of the federal government was only reluctantly, and gradually accepted. Despite this upheaval, the introduction of steam power ushered in interstate commerce on a grand scale by rail and steam ship. Commerce that would be difficult if not impossible under the old *Articles of Confederation*.

Previously, under the old articles, The United States had no means to enforce it's policies nor protect it's interests. Now things were different. In April and May of eighteen hundred five, a combined land and sea force of United States Navy and Marines along with hired mercenaries launched an attack on the pirate held North African city of Derne. The result was an overwhelming U.S. Victory.

Not many years later the British were having a problem keeping The Royal Navy fully staffed during their conflict with France. Their solution was to start impressing sailers, *(kidnapping)*, off American ships at gunpoint. After numerous protests, etc., The United States of America finally declared war on Great Britain in eighteen hundred twelve thus the name,

The War of Eighteen Twelve. We did not acquit ourselves to any
spectacular effect, however our country demonstrated that we
have become a real nation; that can and will act to defend it's
interests at home and abroad.

Nevertheless, our Constitution was written for a different
American public than that of today. Women, non white persons,
those who were deemed insufficiently educated, those who were
thought to have too little property or funds to pay sufficient
taxes were not considered full citizens. Slavery was an accepted
way of life in most of the country, both socially and legally.
Census taking was stipulated by the Constitution but people of
color were to be counted as three fifths of a white person also
as stipulated by the Constitution.

Our great national document as it was originally ratified
had no guarantee of a citizen's right to vote. Elections were
left up to the states. Although the Constitution originally
prohibited any religious requirement for holding any federal
office, there was no prohibition against religious requirements
for voting. Some states did, in fact, have such requirements.
This is because the federal government originally had nothing to
do with elections. All elections were under the aegis of the
separate states. In fact, in the beginning, some states selected
their senators by voting only in their individual state
legislatures; leaving the public out completely. It wasn't until
nineteen hundred thirteen and the passing of the seventeenth
amendment that United States Senators were required to be

selected by popular vote rather than a vote by state
legislature.

Presidential elections are a modern American phenomenon. In
the original Constitution, the framers felt that with such a
mixed ethnic population, especially with the enormous slave
population confusing things further, the public could not be
trusted to select the President. They, therefore, came up with a
bizarre plan in which each state's legislature would select a
number of non office holding people equal to the number of
representatives and senators that the state had in Congress.
These people called electors actually vote for both President
and vice President. As originally written, there is no specific
right to vote in the Constitution. The selection of both members
of Congress as well as United States Senators is left up to the
states. Each state can choose the rules for electing their
representatives or choose to select them by means other than
election.

The Civil War created great social change. Human bondage in
our country was of course ended with a blood bath. The concept
of union forever, of one contiguous country was permanently
established with the same blood bath. Other changes came about
as well. Rail transportation began extending all over the
country. President Lincoln fomented the work on the transcontinental railroad. Rail transport development came about from
agreements between the rail companies and the federal government
as to acquisition of rights of way among other matters; an

149

impossibility before the existence of federal authority.

Creative entrepreneurs began developing industries that together grew into world leading American industrial might. But creating this industrial empire came with staggering social problems that brought new upheavals to the land.

There grew an epidemic of public abuses. Bad medicine, adulterated and unsanitary foods, dangerous and unhealthy workplaces, overworked, underpaid and bullied workers were common across the country. American banks, and other financial institutions were frequently devising schemes to bilk the public. Mostly under Theodore Roosevelt's administration the government took action to regulate foods, drugs, labor, banking and other vital public concerns in order to protect the people. The days of unrestricted capitalism ended. But not without great conflict and strife.

Powerful people tried to shape public opinion with their great economic influence. One of the strategies they devised to do this was to virtually buy the presidency of William McKinley. McKinley was an active advocate of policies friendly to their business interests. While McKinley was friendly towards big business interests the governor of New York State was not. He was speaking about putting controls on the business practices and growth of the enormous corporations and banks called, "*trusts*".

Their strategy was to silence Roosevelt by urging McKinley to select him as his running mate. Because the vice presidency was considered to be an irrelevancy from which no one was ever heard, they thought him to be silenced. Their plan worked. However, shortly after President McKinley's inauguration, he was assassinated. When Roosevelt came into office, the powers that be found him to be incorruptible and stubborn in his beliefs. He went after big business with a vengeance and took steps to protect the public.

Now, more than a hundred years later, there is no such superman like TR to defend the public. However, we are not the same public as in nineteen hundred one.

Through the electronic media of radio, television and the internet, the public is getting much more information at a much faster rate about political issues and candidates. A far greater number of Americans have college degrees. Many more without degrees have at least some college credit. We are no longer a public so easily duped. Our population has lived under and grown to depend on government agencies and regulation to prevent the dangers and abuses of the past. We are growing to expect fairness as well as efficiency from today's government.

However, as the American public has grown more sophisticated and worldly, so have the wealthy and powerful. Using more modern and subtle techniques to achieve the same ends as their predecessors from the nineteenth and early twentieth centuries, they have, through their financial power, bought the services of politicians in both houses of Congress.

Those in possession of economic power have not only

influenced election results, but have caused legislation to be passed that furthers their special interests and blocked passage of many other bills that would not be so favorable to them. One of the countless examples of this is the pledge never to raise taxes that was signed by the conservative legislators in Congress. This was done at the behest of a conservative lobbyist in the employ of powerful economic groups. This single example of governmental corruption has resulted in cuts to vital services for lower and middle income people in order to perpetuate tax breaks for the very wealthy.

Conservative politicians, through the donated funds of their benefactors, can repeat distorted, exaggerated, and often untrue policies and positions. By using bought and paid for pundits and politicians to use their almost limitless donated funds to endlessly repeat accusations and ideas that are in conflict with the financial good of the country, they have convinced large segments of the electorate to vote against their own self interest.

Powerful and wealthy groups have used weaknesses in the Constitution to disenfranchise elements in the electorate that they feel will not vote their way. They do this by using their bought and paid for state legislatures and governors to pass restrictive voting laws in those states that they paid for.

Not surprisingly, this influence on elections and voting rights has had a deleterious effect on our nation. While the very wealthy have seen their income and power rise to unprecedented heights, the resources of the middle and lower income segments of society have been shrinking dramatically. Our country, whose power and influence around the globe was at one time as great as any world power ever was, is also shrinking. Our influence is nowhere near what it once was and it is common to hear about America in decline. The most powerful and successful industrial complex on earth is being rapidly eclipsed by The Peoples Republic of China.

Many articles of our Constitution have become obsolete or moot as the years have gone by. Due to changes in the mores and customs of the population; due to the different ethnic backgrounds of today's electorate and due to the tremendous difference technology has created in life today, constitutional change is needed once more.

It has been shown here that the United States has come into being as a world power that provides the opportunity for a comfortable life as well as personal liberty for it's citizens, through upheaval and change. After each upheaval in our history, life and liberty improved.

Many would argue that dramatic constitutional change will damage our government. Many would, I think, be fearful of a federal autocracy growing out of any effective change. These arguments, I fear, would be repeated endlessly in the media by those funded by the wealthy minority. Nevertheless, this current downward trend in our country's fortunes must be reversed through basic governmental changes. The people must have control over their own government through free and fair elections.

XVII

The decisions selecting congressional representatives and senators as well as President and vice President have always been made under the authority of the various states. This has resulted in the abuses and chaos of fifty different sets of election law. Various states have passed voting requirements that serve no other purpose than to make it difficult for some segments of the population to vote. The restrictions are designed to limit the voting of those parts of the electorate that the party in power feels will vote for the opposition.

The recent Supreme court decisions on campaign funding have resulted in state run elections for federal positions being bought with huge political contributions by the extremely wealthy.

Recently, also, the Supreme Court has ruled that the Voting Rights Act is in part obsolete because of the gains made by minorities in the political arena. Mostly, it seems, that the election of President Obama has triggered this decision.

The result of this last court action has resulted in egregious legislation by the North Carolina government to make voting difficult if not impossible for various segments of the state's population. They have made a requirement to insist on special identification documents that are hard for the elderly to obtain They are now requiring college students to leave their schools to travel home to vote. They have made it impossible for those who just turn eighteen years old to vote by requiring registration to be done long before the date of the election. All this and more was done, they say, to prevent voter fraud. In the last election in North Carolina there was only one case of voter fraud!

Curiously, the demographics in North Carolina and other states that are now facing voting restrictions are those that tend to vote for the party in the state that favors the opposition. While it is true that these anti democracy bills affect the citizens of these restrictive states only, these people are citizens of the United States of America and should have the right to vote without restriction.

Because of this and the fact that these elected positions are for the federal government, they should meet federal standards and fall under the authority of the national government. The mechanism for doing this already exists. It is the Federal Elections Commission.

The Federal Elections Commission, (FEC), was brought into existence by Congress to supervise and enforce the Federal Election Campaign Act. This act attempted to correct election abuses that have plagued the country for decades. As far back as the administration of Theodore Roosevelt, Congress had recognized this problem and began to pass statutes to limit the influence of the wealthy minority upon federal election results. Congress legislated controls on campaign financing as well as enforcing some degree of transparency. This finally resulted in the Federal Election Campaign Act.

The recent Supreme Court ruling in the Citizens United case has nullified most of the legislative efforts to control election abuse. The court decided that limiting the spending of money for political campaigns was unconstitutional. In order to correct our flawed federal election procedures, we must once again amend our eighteenth century constitution.

The first step necessary is to place all federal elections under one authority. That authority could be a revitalized FEC. This commission would be the sole authority over the conduct of federal elections. The authority would decide on all voter registration details including I.D. requirements, early, late and absentee registration, proof of citizenship and any other pertinent details. Election procedures as well as ballot counting procedures would fall under the same authority.

This means that all ballots in all states would be similar. All voting equipment would be the same. *(No hanging chads)* Exit poll procedures would be uniform. Equipment and procedures for tallying the vote would be the same as would be the requirements for all people involved in running the election. Now all federal government positions would be selected by public popular vote. This should include the presidency and vice presidency which are now decided by a weird procedure employing a weird body of people called, The Electoral College.

As previously discussed, the framers of our constitution did not trust the public with the election of the national executive. Actually, they did not specify general elections for anything. The selection of congressional representatives and senators was left up to the legislative bodies of the individual states. Some states held elections for this and some did not.

The selection of President and Vice President is the responsibility of the members of the Electoral College in each of the several states. The states choose a set of electors for each qualified candidate running for office in their individual state. The selection of electors is decided by the states in a manner that varies from state to state. The states are allotted a number of electors equal to the number of representatives and senators that they have in Congress. The public votes to choose electors, not the candidates. The electors are the ones who vote for the President, not the people.

When the election proceeds according to Hoyle, the electors vote for the candidate the public has chosen them to vote for. However, there is no law that compels this. Although it has happened that an elector has cast his vote against the candidate he was supposed to support, no elector has ever been prosecuted for doing so as it violates no current law..

In almost every state the winner of the popular vote wins the state's electors. No matter what the popular vote results, the winner, even by the narrowest margin, gets all the state's electors. On occasion this has resulted in a President being in office that the majority of Americans did not vote for. Perhaps the most common, and therefore, the most serious consequence of the electoral college is the all or nothing allotment of

158

electors. Today it is possible to predict the electoral vote outcome in most states, leaving just a handful of states where the outcome is in doubt. It is in these key states where most of the electioneering takes place. It is in these states where the bulk of the advertising money is spent and it is in these few states where the candidates make personal appearances. This is because the voter's ballots are more important and votes have a greater impact on the outcome of the election in these few key states. In our democracy today, everyone's vote is not equal!

A twenty eighth amendment to the Constitution could take care of nationalizing all our federal elections by placing them under the regulations and authority of the FEC.

A twenty ninth amendment could establish basic constitutional requirements for all federal elections.

With a twenty eighth amendment, or its equivalent, as to be proposed here, the problem of fifty different election rules for the same campaign will be solved.

The first four constitutional election regulations in this proposed twenty ninth amendment will solve many of our federal campaign problems as well as finally getting rid of the anti democratic electoral college.

As stated often here, our greatest problem with elections is the problem that is crippling the government. It is the problem that causes our government officials to act in the interest of a microscopically small, powerful minority instead of the majority of the American electorate and their vital concerns.

The influence of money on elections increases the time that can be spent campaigning. Reducing the time spent campaigning limits the opportunity to spend large funds.

It is through regulating both the time allotted for running elections and the funds available to run them that can clean up, and streamline our election process. Such streamlined elections will get our government working efficiently and in the interest of the American people.

Political activity today is being funded by unrestricted and essentially unidentified donations to PACs, *(political action committees)*. When donors wish to support a candidate by using a large, politically influential donation, they can give to a super PAC. By doing this, they can donate any amount they want and not worry about revealing their identity or intensions until after the race has been decided. This will permit the special interests to get their candidate elected and thusly their personal agenda passed into law. To stop this damage to democratic, representative government, private political donations must be limited and political action committees must be abolished.

Donations from individual voters would go directly to candidates. Limits on donations must be set for every individual as well as limits for corporations, unions and other interested groups.

Keying the maximum permitted political donation by

individuals to the national average per capita income for the election year, will go a long way to limit abuses. In the year 2007 the average per capita income was $38,600. If donations had been restricted to ten percent of this national average income, then the maximum personal political contribution would have been no more than $3,860 for a federal election in the following year, 2008. Group and corporate contributions could have been limited to five times the average per capita income.

Using 2007 average per capita income data, the maximum permissible group or corporate donation would have been $193,000 under this plan, for the following year, 2008. This seems to be a large permissible donation, however, for large corporations it is a mere drop in the bucket; especially considering the multi million dollars they spend on political influence today.

Of course these are proposed maximum limits. A group or an individual can contribute less or nothing. To promote public donations and involvement, tax exemptions can be offered to defray the cost of individual contributions. While this scheme would help to reduce election abuse and limit the influence of the privileged on government, it would not generate sufficient funds to run even a greatly shortened campaign.

Adding to the funding available for politics the government would be required to add a per vote bonus to each qualified political party. The greater the number of votes a party can attract, the greater their share of government funding. How these funds are distributed and spent would be determined by the party provided that is spent exclusively during the FEC election campaign schedule. This method would provide additional funds to those who most appeal to the electorate. With this type of system it is likely that numerous political parties will be created.

Multiple parties would be more responsive to new ideas as well as being able to more accurately reflect public opinion. Under the present two party system the diverse views of the public often find no voice.

Today's Republican party refers to itself as the party of small government. Their membership and Republican elected leaders speak of getting government out of people's lives. To this end they fight to prevent many government rules and regulations and agitate to eliminate and weaken those regulations that are already in affect. Yet this same party is passing laws bringing government into people's social and private lives; passing laws and regulations that they claim to be against. They strive to pass laws regulating marriage, birth control and other social issues that bring government regulations into citizen's bedrooms. If a voter believes in small government and low taxes, the only party that person can vote for is one that pushes governmental social intrusions.

Using this proposed system of per vote financing, diverse political parties can accumulate start up money for their next campaign. Political funding would therefore be provided by the decisions of the voting public through their donations and by their actual votes.

Candidates will run as selected by their political parties. A candidate that choses to run for office as an independent, will have to run as the candidate of an independent party. Political parties must qualify as legitimate political parties by means of public petition.

Required to obtain a petition of at least thirty thousand citizen signatures, a fledgling party would receive government start up money of five dollars per each of the first thirty thousand qualified signatures. The per signature start up funds can be adjusted to the economic reality of the times. After this the party would have to be self supporting or allowed to fail. Once it has achieved its position as a qualified party, and has been given start up money, it can only be funded by the FEC through the per vote bonus system and regulated dontions. Funds accrued by political parties may only be spent on political campaigns and may not be invested for gain.

This type of election financial control should provide better government and fairer elections. Good government, however, demands attention from elected officials. Our officials cannot run the government and make effective decisions if they must spend more than a year electioneering which is often the case now.

The limitations of the proposed funding system should serve to shorten political campaigns considerably. Time limits must nevertheless be imposed to be sure that elected officials are not distracted from the duties of their offices.

Electioneering should be shortened by the government to no more than two months for every election for federal office or for national referenda. This can be accomplished by both restricting the distribution of campaign funds to the two months campaign schedule, and by prohibiting the spending of any funds except during the campaign period.

No funds would be permitted to be spent on political advertising or publicity before the date of the government announced beginning of the campaign. Parties would be free to select candidates for office through primary elections, caucus, or any other means that the party membership and leadership selects. The primary process would be regulated to take place only during the two month election period by using the same spending restrictions as in general elections.

Primary campaigns and candidate selection funding would come from party coffers of money left over from previous donations and previous government per vote funding. All political activity would be restricted to candidates and political parties alone. No committee to re-elect, no American Petroleum Institute, no citizens for a cleaner anything would be allowed to purchase any political advertising.

What differentiates political from commercial advertisement? As an example, advertisements for the burning of coal in America can be examined. If the message is one that urges the viewer or reader to purchase coal or coal burning equipment or service, then that would be a commercial message and would not be subject to FEC regulation. If, however, there was no obvious intent to promote sales, but rather a message urging the public to support the passage or defeat of any candidate or government policy or regulation then a hearing could be held to determine if the advertisement was political or not. If, after a fair hearing, it was determined to be political, then the ad would have to be pulled off the air or no longer distributed if printed. This would serve to prevent powerful special interests from influencing public elections and government policy.

These constitutional changes proposed here are neither new nor revolutionary nor even untried. Similar election practices have been used successfully for years in other democratic societies. With these new election law changes in place, the influence of a tiny minority on national elections will be greatly reduced. Reduced also will be the damaging influence of the special interest lobbies. Although they will not likely disappear, the lobbyists will not be able to promise political support to officials, because no promise of large campaign donations could be made or fulfilled.

XVIII

Much here has been proposed as Constitutional change. What could such amendments look like? A twenty eighth and twenty ninth amendment could be worded in many ways. For example:

XXVIII. To insure fair and democratic elections for federal offices nationwide, all such elections and election campaigns shall be funded by and regulated by the Federal Elections Commission. This will include Congressional and Senatorial elections. The Commission will be responsible to assure that elections and election campaigns are run and funded according to the election rules and standards as set forth in Amendment Twenty Nine.

XXIX. The Federal Election Commission shall be charged with enforcing the following election procedural and fiscal regulations, standards and guidelines.

1. All candidate for all federal offices, including President and Vice President shall be direct public elections decided by popular vote.

2. All elections and campaigns, for any federal office including both general and primary efforts must begin and end within a sixty day time limit as scheduled by the FEC.

3. All election ballots, voting machines and voting procedures as well as allowances for special

circumstance shall be strictly controlled by the FEC.

4. All campaign financing is to fall under the following FEC election funding rules.

   a. Donations from individuals shall be limited to ten percent of the national average income for the year preceding the election and donated to the candidate's parties directly.

   b. Corporate and group political contributions are limited to five times the national average individual income for the year preceding the election and donated to the candidate's party directly.

   c. Income tax deductions shall be permitted for political contributions by individuals.

   d. Each licensed political party would receive a bonus payment from the FEC based strictly on the number of votes received during the election. The per vote bonus value will be set annually by the governing board of the commission. The funds will be provided to the FEC budget by the United States Senate.

e. No political spending of any kind from any source either before or after the sixty day election period is permitted.

f. Political spending for events, electronic media advertising or publicity as well as for print media advertising is permitted only by the candidates or their party.

g. Legitimate political spending for advertising or publicity by a candidate or qualified political party as well as any fund raising for individual contributions may take place only during the sixty day election schedule.

1. No political funds may be spent or invested by parties, candidates or elected officials except for political campaigns during the FEC campaign schedule.

5. All political parties must be licensed by the FEC to be permitted to function in FEC elections.

a. Newly formed parties must provide a

thirty thousand voter petition for party
license.

b. Final party licensing will be decided by
the governing body of the commission.

The Commission shall be empowered to react to violations of
these election regulations by the imposition of fines as well as
the authority to invalidate an election result, or a candidate's
eligibility or even a party's license.

XIX

These changes to our national document are profound. They abridge some of our liberties to permit others to grow. They limit the freedoms of the extremely wealthy and powerful to invest their money and influence in order to unduly bend national policies to their own ends. Thusly, we can assure that our government will do what it was originally intended to do, act in the interest of the general population.

There are many who would decry these Constitutional changes. Do they realize how much our venerable Constitution has already changed? Do they realize that the law of our land was written for a culture and technology that hasn't existed for more than two hundred twenty years? Do they realize how much of this document was written to address problems of that long extinct society? Do they realize how much of it was written to protect the nation from an incursion or political take over by a monarchy? Do they realize that our founders wrote unequal representation into the very fabric of our government? Clearly our Constitution was written for a long vanished world.

We have a senate that is comprised of two senators from each state. This was done as the Constitution was being framed. Small states fearing they would be overwhelmed by the larger states with greater representation, resisted unification and the drafting of a constitution. This fomented the idea of two houses of Congress. One, The House of Representatives, with representation from the states based on population. The other,

The Senate with two senators per state so that in the senate, each state, large and small, would have an equal voice. When this was in acted we were a confederation of member nation/states that were looking for compromises to unify us.

We are no longer such a confederation. We are one nation. In our one, great nation, we like to think we are all citizens with an equal voice in our representative democracy. However, even though this is what we like to think, as shown, it is not reality.

If our government works precisely as it should; exactly as the framers designed it to work; there would be, nevertheless, unequal representation in Congress for our citizens. This is because there are two senators for every state. States like Pennsylvania, New York or Texas have the same two senators each as states like Rhode Island, Delaware or Nebraska that have only a fraction of their population. We seem more concerned with the rights of the fifty semi states that make up our union rather than the rights of each of the citizens of our one nation.

The weakness in our government's Constitution is readily apparent in today's headlines. Our United States Senate, the representatives of the people, voted down a federal requirement for background checks for purchasers of firearms. The bill lost in the senate vote despite the fact that almost ninety percent of the American People support such legislation. The bill lost in the senate vote despite the fact that it drew the majority vote winning fifty four to forty six in a winning loss!

It seems that our senate has decided without any Constitutional justification that in order to prevent a filibuster they would require a winning vote to be at least sixty. Our sacred Constitution seems to apply only when it can be used to reduce taxes or make money for they very, very wealthy.

Despite the fact that our Constitution was written for a group of separate nations as a unifying as well as a governing document, despite the fact that it was written for an experimental democracy in a world of powerful monarchies, despite all the amendments that attempt to modernize it, our Constitution was the first representative democracy in the modern world! It was the document that had the greatest influence in nations worldwide than almost any other document in human history!

During the years that the Constitution was being written and ratified, the influential and powerful nations of the world were governed mostly by absolute monarchies. After years passed, it was becoming apparent that the American experiment of representative democracy was actually working. This generated public pressure in many nations forcing royals to share power with an elected governing body. Many monarchs, under public pressure, gave up all real authority; turning all power over to an elected representative body. Still others held on to power and privilege until they were removed by force in a revolution.

Through the years many republics have come and gone. Some

worked quite well and some were horrible failures. Some consider themselves to be monarchies and have all the trappings that go with a royal family and an aristocracy. Yet their countries are governed by elected representatives and their citizens enjoy all the personal liberties expected in modern society.

Through the years from the ratification of the American Constitution to the present day, many forms of representative democracy have been tried. Many variations of a parliamentary form of government as well as a presidential form of democracy have been tried and have succeeded.

All the experience around the world forming many different types of republican, democratic government can provide numerous examples for us that can guide us in modifying and re-writing our Constitution. Just like our Constitution provided guidance, direction and inspiration for so many countries to follow, we can use the experience of other nations to improve our government by bringing it up to date.

XX

The weaknesses and obsolescence of sections of our Constitution have been part of it from the very start. In order for the states to ratify our national document, it had to be amended before a vote to ratify could even be taken. These first ten amendments, called, "The Bill of Rights", were adopted in order that both the citizenry and the various states could feel comfortable with their new government.

Even these first Constitutional changes are somewhat obsolete now. Specifically, the second amendment, which is so much under discussion these days, is outdated. As many parts of the document, the second amendment was written for a country that no longer exists. Our country is no longer protected by a militia of any kind and hasn't been since the war of eighteen twelve. We need a re-write!

The U.S.A. is governed by an almost unbelievable redundancy of fifty one governments regulating and legislating similar if not identical things. Previously, the myriad of election laws in the various states were discussed, including the injustice of elections in states where religious, ethnic or racial biases have effected election procedure.

Not discussed, however, was, in addition to federal laws and regulations, the existence of fifty different health regulations, fifty different sets of banking regulations, fifty different sets of insurance guide lines, fifty different consumer protection laws and so on ad nausea.

Of course, doing anything about the redundancies and injustices of all these duplicated governments would foment a huge cry in protest of what would be termed a gross violation of state's rights.

But do state's rights really exist in our country? Can the individual states wage war against a foreign power? Can individual states mint their own coin? They can't even run their own postal services. These aren't real states. That most of them call themselves states doesn't mean that they are. The only actual, real, fully functioning state in all this is the United States of America. What do state's rights really mean?

There is an example of state's rights carried to a logical conclusion in our history. It obviously was the civil war. That conflict made clear that state's rights were other words for the dissolution of our nation.

When there is an argument supporting state's rights, it would seem at first to be an argument in support of liberty and justice. However, if enough thought is given to this term, the question arrises, who is gaining rights and from whom are they being gained?

There are some examples of rights that were held by the states. Rights that they lost because of federal action initiated to foment personal freedom of American citizens.

States at one time had the right to pass laws that enforced human bondage and the sale of people as a commodity. States at one time had the right to select people to serve as United

States Senators any way they wished until the federal government required public elections. States could and in some circumstances, still can, run public elections any way they see fit. Some states now are beginning a new pogrom against women by restricting their opportunities for adequate and affordable medical care. States have been persecuting the gay community for years and only recently have some of them began to lift some of their oppressive restrictions. Some states have opted out of the federal Affordable Care Act and are leaving their public in a vacuum of dangerously inadequate health care insurance.

When the Constitution was first ratified we were a group of thirteen different countries. Our national document was designed to bring us together as much as it was to govern.

We are no longer separate nations held together by a document. We are one nation! When the civil war first broke out General Robert E. Lee was offered a command in the United States Army. General Lee not only refused the command, he resigned his commission in the U.S. military because he couldn't fight for any organization that would invade his Virginia. In his papers the General made it clear that he was first and always a Virginian. There are many of us that love our home states but think of ourselves as first and always an American. Our country is not Virginia, nor Colorado, nor Kansas, nor New Jersey, but the United States of America.

XXI

Any government is really only as effective, benevolent and just as it is perceived to be. When a government is trusted it can govern well and accomplish much. This has been demonstrated by the United States Government during World War Two.

During the post war years of the nineteen fifties the population supported and trusted their government as well as other large national organizations. This lead to great accomplishments. General Motors made more vehicles every year than all foreign manufacturers combined. The popular opinion was, "What's good for GM is good for the country." The total assets and capital wealth of AT&T exceeded that of many nations.

Our federal government made the interstate highway system a reality. Later that same government formed the National Aeronautics and Space Administration which put men on the moon and brought them home safely; a jaw dropping, stupendous accomplishment.

As the years went by the effectiveness and the accomplishments of the United States government began to wain as the distrust of the government grew. The ability of the nation to use the coordinated efforts of government and private industry to achieve dramatic and useful public goals was and is stifled by the apathy and disinterest of a suspicious population.

The distrust of large corporations stems from the scandals that grew out of what has been believed to be corporate greed.

Both Congress and the President are broadly perceived to be operating exclusively for the benefit of corporations and the extremely wealthy. There is ample evidence to support this widely held belief. Suspicion grows because of the structure of our tax code and even by what many consider the intentional incomprehensibility of it all.

It was these kinds of inequities that were the seeds that sprouted into the Marxist revolution of the last century. It seems unlikely that communism will rise again, but angry people can make very quick and very profound changes.

To bring public trust back to government, inequities must be addressed. They can be addressed by redrafting our national document into a modern constitution.

Today, the meaningless language of the second amendment to the Constitution has resulted in what can only be called wholesale slaughter in our major cities. There must be included in the body of a new Constitution a simple and understandable article that would spell out clearly a modern version of the right to bear arms. This article of the revised constitution would regulate the nationwide distribution of handguns, while permitting the private, unregulated ownership of non automatic rifles and shotguns.

While the public is represented in Congress, we are not represented fairly. As long as the senate is made up of two senators from each state irregardless of the state's population we have unequal representation. A new national document could

178

reform Congress partly to insure fair representation.

The federal tax code must be rewritten in plain, understandable language. It should have a minimum of loopholes, no tax shelters and everyone forced to pay their fair share. The code should be written into our new national document. The fact that our current, supposedly progressive tax code allows extremely wealthy individuals to pay a far lower tax rate than their office workers, and the added fact that some wealthy and successful corporations have at times paid no income tax whatever, has infuriated the public and has been one of the causes of the Occupy Wall Street movement.

There are progressive states and conservative states, but the political climate of a state's governor and/or legislature should not impact the personal liberties and opportunities of their citizens who are first and foremost citizens of the United States of America. The right of a woman to get medical care in Tennessee should be the same as a woman from Massachusetts. The procedure to register to vote should be the same in Pennsylvania as it is in California. It should be no more difficult to obtain a firearm in New York as it is in Florida. However, it should be impossible to obtain an illegal firearm anywhere in the USA. States have no rights! States have powers and our many, "states", have far too much. They have the power to limit personal freedoms of law abiding citizens of the USA that live within their borders.

XXII

Equality before the law has been an American ideal for years. Unfortunately it is a completely unrealized ideal. Both in criminal and civil law the wealthy and powerful in society can use their power and wealth to gain great advantage in almost any legal situation.

In civil actions the wealthy can hire attorneys to file endless briefs and challenges for years. Thus wearing down their less well heeled opponents. Often in cases of law suits against powerful corporations, the average person is often forced to settle for amounts that are only a fraction of the damages they actually suffered.

Worse yet, is the situation in the criminal courts. When the accused is sufficiently well to do, there is means to hire the best legal defense, the best, and most expensive attorneys, the best team of private investigators and what ever else they can bring to bear including expert witnesses, private medical examiners and laboratories. The middle income accused has only the help of the public defender who is often not particularly well paid and often rather disinterested in such a non lucrative case.

A revised and updated Constitution can address these issues far better than a patchwork of amendments to the current obsolete document that governs us today. The legal quicksand of both Senate and House procedural and voting rules which mostly exist outside of any article of our Constitution must be addressed by a new document that can effectively deal with issues of gerrymandering and filibuster.

By adopting and using these constitutionally unwritten procedures, minorities in Congress have thwarted the will of the people and have been working against the common good. As in the recent lack of congressional action in instituting background checks for firearms purchasers; the will of the people had little impact in Congress. Our current system of unregulated political funding will allow special interests tremendous power to short circuit any attempt at constitutional reform.

XXIII

The realistic likelihood of any sort of redrafting of the Constitution is microscopically small. The only way that such a change in government seems at all possible is with a different population of politicians in Congress.

To make such a reshaping of our government would take politicians who are more concerned with their place in history rather than their position on the economic ladder.

As things are today, the goal of the overwhelming number of congressmen and senators is to keep their elected positions at all costs. When politicians' terms are finally over, they can start to earn real money by lobbying for gas company fracking schemes, or oil pipe lines or agricultural corporate interests or wherever the big bucks are.

To get honest, representatives who are interested in actual honest, innovative, and efficient government, the enormous profit motive in politics must be eliminated. The way to remove the enormous profit is to agitate for Constitutional amendments similar to those discussed here.

The myriad of legitimate complaints voiced by the Occupy Movement and others, is mostly addressed by the amendments discussed here or similar Constitutional changes. This can result in a free, fair and much more independent government. A government that can work towards correcting all that had been done to benefit the few at the cost of the many.

Perhaps a start with election reform can preclude a new

more modern and relevant Constitution.

With this new Constitution could come real health reform.

With this new Constitution could come real legal reform.

With this new Constitution could come a great rebuilding and updating of American cities and infrastructure.

With this new Constitution could come a new flowering of American education and technological acumen.

With this Constitution a new dynamic and growing middle income population can succeed.

With this new Constitution the government of the rich and powerful, by the rich and powerful and, increasingly, for the rich and powerful, shall fade from this earth; and the government of, by and for the people, will begin another new and world leading example of good government and working democracy in action!

* * *

183